# BEST HENS FOR YOU

## CHOOSING BREEDS
## FOR THE GARDEN

## The Author and Editor

*Charlotte Popescu has kept hens in her garden for many years as family pets. She also had her own bantams when growing up in Oxfordshire. Married with three boys, Charlotte lives the lifestyle that she writes about: keeping hens; growing vegetables and summer fruits; gathering fruits of the hedgerow for jams and jellies.*

*Building on the success of her book: **Hens in the Garden, Eggs in the Kitchen**, in this new book Charlotte explores which breeds will be most suitable for a family garden.*

*Charlotte Popescu is the daughter of Christine Pullein-Thompson, writer of pony stories and grand daughter of Joanna Cannan, originator of the genre of pony books and well known novelist. Charlotte has published poems by her great aunt, May Wedderburn Cannan in a book called **The Tears of War**, under her married name, Charlotte Fyfe.*

# BEST HENS FOR YOU

## CHOOSING BREEDS
## FOR THE GARDEN

By

**Charlotte Popescu**

**CAVALIER PAPERBACKS**

© Charlotte Popescu 2006

Illustrations by Roger Phillippo

Published by Cavalier Paperbacks 2006
Reprinted 2007, 2008

Cavalier Paperbacks
Burnham House,
Upavon,
Wilts SN9 6DU

www.cavalierpaperbacks.co.uk

ISBN 9781899470327

Printed and bound in Great Britain by Baskerville Press,
Salisbury, Wilts

# CONTENTS

# INTRODUCTION

Keeping hens is Britain's fastest growing hobby. Many people are choosing to keep a few hens in the garden especially for the benefit of fresh eggs collected straight from the nest box. Hens look attractive in the garden and they make great pets for the family. Children love collecting the eggs and my three boys love watching Mother Hen looking after a new brood of chicks.

 The most difficult decisions about keeping hens are what breeds to choose, how many, how big and what colour. Nearly every breed of large fowl has been created in a smaller version, known as miniature fowl or bantams. Bantams are smaller than hens and will eat less but will lay smaller eggs. However if you are limited on space these are definitely an option to consider.

 There are a lot of hybrid hens on the market with new names. These have been developed by crossing breeds to develop a hen that will primarily lay more eggs in one year that a traditional pure breed would. They are also being bred to look attractive in your garden. However these hybrids won't lay so many eggs after their first two years and in that sense they are not unlike battery hens. The other disadvantage to the hybrids is that although cockerels are available for those who really want them, they don't breed true so you cannot reproduce the hybrids yourself. The Black Rock hybrids are bred by a sole breeder in Scotland and his agents only sell hens to the public.

Cross breeds, which can be a mixture of all sorts of breeds, tend to be the hardiest, live the longest and keep laying the longest, even if erratically. Cross breeds are also the easiest hens to name. If you buy hybrids or pure breeds of one type you can name them but will have real problems telling them apart as they will all look the same. People often want to know which breeds are tame and most suitable for the garden and which breeds lay the most eggs. However, quite a lot depends on the strains within a breed. For example, I have had letters from people about their tame Leghorns which traditionally are liable to be nervous and flighty.

Flighty behaviour can very much depend on management – if you spend time with your hens, feeding them, watching them and handling them, they are likely to become quite tame.

Every bird has its own individual personality, regardless of its breed which is why I have been collecting anecdotes from owners about their hens.

As a general rule lightweight breeds that lay white eggs are more skittish than heavy breeds that lay brown eggs. If you want dark brown eggs from the traditional breeds you should go for Maranses,

Welsummers or Barnevelders. If you want pretty bantams go for gold, silver or blue-laced Wyandottes. If you want pretty bantams which are also reliable egg layers go for Sussexes. If you want small cuddly bantams suitable for young children to handle, go for Pekins (the ones with the feathery legs) but they go broody rather frequently. If you want blue/turquoise eggs go for Araucanas from South America, but they may be flighty. If your main priority is to get eggs every day, go for Black Rocks or Bovans Nera. If you want to give your hens names, don't buy four hens of exactly the same breed and colour or you will have problems distinguishing them.

If you can, try to buy at least two of any one breed as chickens seem to be happier hanging out with a friend of the same breed. I have a lone Araucana and a lone Poland bantam – both are very wild and the Poland in particular is very skittish.

# BASIC FACTS FOR THOSE NEW TO KEEPING HENS

You don't need a cockerel for your hens to lay eggs, unlike a wild bird, which only lays an egg if fertilised by a male. Cocks can be fierce, they will wake you and your neighbours crowing at dawn so if you don't wish to breed from your hens, don't buy one. It is probably best to start off with four hens. Later on, you can buy fertilised eggs and put them under a broody hen, but be aware that you will hatch cocks as well as hens. The best time to buy your hens is in the Spring at point of lay (POL) when they are 18 - 22 weeks old. Look in Country Smallholding magazine. Prices vary from £10 to £40 each for pure breeds and £5 to £12 for hybrids and cross breeds.

## Management

The minimum space needed for four bantams is 4 x 2 metres, 12 x 6 feet. You will need a weatherproof house which you can buy or build, with perches and nest boxes, a drinker, feeder and mixed poultry corn or layers pellets and green stuff if you want truly yellow eggs. They will need as much access to open spaces of grass as possible. They will peck at the growing tips of grass, dandelion leaves, chick weed, in fact almost anything green. They will also love spinach and lettuce – you will soon discover what they like best. Mine love spaghetti (which reminds them of worms) cooked rice, bananas and bread. Don't forget that if your hens are enclosed they will need grit to aid digestion and you may have been told that they need oyster shells for strong egg shells. In fact the extra calcium for egg shells is now provided in the mixed feed that you can buy from your local merchant.

If you have a large garden and want your hens to be completely free range you need only a hen house in which to close them up in the evening. As well as providing interest and colour, hens can be a help in the garden, breaking up the soil after you have dug it, foraging for pests and producing droppings, a great fertiliser. My bantams love following me around when I'm digging, grabbing worms from under my fork. However they will scratch in the borders, eat your lettuces and take dust baths so you should protect your prized vegetables and plants.

Beware if your hens are free range because foxes usually strike at dusk or dawn and they may well kill all your poultry on one visit (urban foxes are the most daring). Dogs can also devastate your flock and cats will kill chicks. You may decide on an enclosed run but make sure it is fox proof by burying 2 metre, 6 foot fences at least a foot into the ground. Electric fencing is a possibility to keep the fox out and I have heard from several people recommending it. If you are in a town, you may have to keep your hens entirely enclosed. An Ark which is attached to a hen house is a good option as it can be moved to fresh grass. You may want to consider the Eglu which is a new type of brightly coloured hen house complete with foxproof run provided by Omlet Ltd.

## Problems

Hens can live for 10 years (or even longer if very lucky) although sometimes they die for no apparent reason. Not all vets will treat sick hens and tend to administer antibiotics which may not work. Problems to look out for are: White crusty legs caused by the scaly leg mite - treat the legs with a proprietary product; Red mites which live and breed in crevices in hen houses and at night run up the chicken's leg and suck blood. They don't live on the bird but can be spotted during the day, red if they have recently sucked blood, or grey if not. Affected birds will stop laying. There are various products on the market available to deal with them; Lice are another problem. Irritating for the bird, they can be treated with louse powder. You should also dust the nest boxes.

If birds are kept too long on the same ground they may need worming with Flubenvet.

# SOME DOS AND DON'TS

Do ask the hen's age and whether she has started laying before you buy - if you buy birds at only a few weeks old, you may not know whether you have hens or cockerels.

Do keep new hens confined for a few days to get used to surroundings.

Do feed plenty of green stuff.

Do watch for bullying and segregate if necessary.

Don't expect your hens to lay all year round. Pure breeds and cross breeds will stop during the winter.

Don't be alarmed when your hens lose a lot of their feathers in the autumn – this is called moulting and happens once a year, hens will usually stop laying during their moult – new feathers grow in place of the old ones surprisingly quickly.

Don't rely on livestock markets for young, healthy birds.

Don't leave food lying around or you'll attract rats.

# CHOOSING YOUR BREEDS

Now for the breeds which I have divided into three sections: Pure Breeds which include large fowl and bantams; Hybrids; Cross Breeds and ex-battery hens.

I have received stories and accounts from people with the more popular breeds especially those common after the Second World War such as Sussexes and Leghorns and also from people who are keeping the currently popular hybrids such as Black Rocks. I am not covering every breed in this book but those that seem most suitable for the garden and a few that are not so suitable but are worth a mention.

## A WORD ON COCKERELS

*Eris from Sussex writes:*

"Some birds are best avoided if you have close neighbours, or even distant neighbours who suffer from nerve problems. If you want to avoid confrontations at all costs, make sure you avoid keeping Guinea Fowl. The continuous calling of the females, sounding for all the world like an un-oiled wheel in perpetual motion, will cause even the most patient neighbours to want to fire up the barbecue for a tasty guinea-fowl roast. And after a few weeks of the noise you will be only too happy to join in the feast!

In general most neighbours seem to prefer the deep mellow tones of a very large cockerel to the turbulent and rather persistent screeching of the bantams. The Croad Langshan (see page 44) has a very deep resonant crow, that many people at shows always comment on as being a 'lovely sound'. Certainly something that can't often be said for most bantam breeds.

If you listen to the sounds of the birds you soon learn that each bird has its own distinctive crow. Only once in over 30 years of keeping birds have I ever owned a cockerel that had, in my opinion the 'perfect' crow. A real 'cock-a-doodle-doo'. Every syllable well placed and delivered with true virtuoso style. This was a large Vorwerk male and listening to his crow was a real pleasure. (For more on Vorwerks see page 102).

Most cockerels make noises that can vary from 'cock-a-warbled-cluck' up to 'doodle-yodel-hick,' with many choices in between.

Many people new to poultry think that the hens are virtually silent, only making the odd happy cluck. Yet a batch of hens startled by a predator can out perform any cockerel when it comes to the decibel stakes! Indeed you will soon learn it is the cockerel that calms the situation by giving an all-clear crow."

# PURE BREEDS

Traditional pure breeds will always breed true; that is the young will resemble their parents. These are available as large fowl but often have miniature versions which we refer to as bantams. There are also some true bantams which don't have large fowl counterparts – these include Pekins, Dutch, Belgian Bearded, Booted, Nankins, Sebrights and Japanese.

All pure breeds are classified as either Hard Feather or Soft Feather and these are sub divided into Heavy, Light and True Bantam breeds. Just to confuse things there is a further classification of Rare Breeds (these are bred in insufficient numbers to enable a Breed Club to be formed).

In this book I am only going to deal with the more popular breeds which you might like to think about for your garden but I am going to include a few rarer breeds which I think are worth considering.

I must emphasise that pure breeds from different breeders may vary in temperament and laying abilities – it is the strain that is important – this is why it is better not to buy from a market where you cannot see where the hens have been living with the rest of the flock.

I once agreed to buy two POL silver-laced Wyandottes over the phone and my husband collected them from Wales. They both died a few months later; one never laid any eggs and the other only laid shell-less eggs.

*Dawn McAllister from High Wycombe, Buckinghamshire writes on her first experiences with pure breeds:*

"A friend of mine asked very casually if I would like her hen house when she moved as she wanted to get a large house and more chickens. I went home to my husband and mentioned in passing that she had offered me her hen house and did he think the kids would enjoy having hens. Before I knew it we had bought the hen house and we were searching for somewhere to purchase chickens. I had a good look on the internet at different breeds but was not really clear about the difference between pure breeds and hybrids. We found a lovely man in Windsor who runs The Garden Hen, on an allotment at the back of his garden. He was very enthusiastic, knowledgeable and helpful and showed us all the pure breeds and gave us lots of information about each one. I really wanted a Silkie, so we got one and we also chose a Leghorn because they are so beautiful and good layers. Our buff Sussex was chosen because she looks like a typical fat hen and our Andalusian was chosen for her beauty.

Looking back at the pictures now at five weeks they definitely were not beautiful hens but at 24 weeks they are now stunning, so if you want pretty hens I'd recommend pure breeds.

## White Leghorn
She is the boss, flighty and have had to clip her wing. Very friendly, easy to handle and has been laying for a month and is laying an egg a day at the moment. Noisy when she has laid.

## Andalusian
Again flighty (so wing clipped). Not quite as friendly as our Leghorn.

## Buff Sussex
Big bird and I'm sure she is not fully grown yet. If there is food she is first there. Again will fly round the garden.

## Silkie
She is beautiful, extremely friendly, everyone loves her. She is bottom of our pecking order and gets very stressed out if separated from the others. She is easy to handle (she is not a bantam), small and easy for children to handle. Obviously not the best of layers but I would have more Silkies.

I warn people that they are addictive. I'm already planning to change my hen house next year so I can have more hens.

*Anne Prideaux from Upavon, Wiltshire writes about her experiences with an assorted flock of pure breeds (Cochin, Buff Orpington and Pekin cockerel and Cochin, Marans, Pekin and Black Rock hens) :*

"It started when we went to buy an old tractor to help keep the grass down in the field where my pony grazed. While my husband discussed technical details, I was busy checking out the chickens. Our friends selling the tractor were moving and would have no space for either tractor or chickens. By the time the tractor deal had been completed I had negotiated the purchase of four hens and suggested a friend may take another four. That left a pair of bantams, who were destined for a breeder and a pair of cockerels, who were destined for the great chicken coop in the sky. I was adamant that I didn't want cockerels....

Excited by our impending new pets, I quickly purchased a book on chickens and set about finding what sort of house they would need. I hadn't at all anticipated what an involved and costly process this would be. However I'd commissioned the building of a house and the chickens were now imminent. The breeder who was supposed to take the pair of bantams hadn't appeared, so I was offered those too. I thought that one little cockerel wouldn't be too bad but I hardened my heart against the two large cockerels. We don't have any close neighbours, but I wasn't too keen on early wake-up calls myself. I told myself firmly that it was essential to be practical when dealing with animals, that it wasn't my problem…. Then my most practical husband decided that it was a shame to leave just two cockerels to meet their fate and persuaded me to take the lot!

The new house finally arrived just hours before we were to pick up the chickens. We had arranged to collect the chickens at dusk, when they were tired and gathering for bed. It will come as no surprise to anyone who has ever tried to move livestock that on the day itself the heavens opened, and it was pitch black by the time we got them home. Trying to transfer them from their boxes in a downpour in the dark was enough to test the strongest of marriages. At one point I found myself shut in the hen-house, in darkness, surrounded by chickens with my husband demanding from outside how many were in there – difficult to know as he had the torch.

However, we safely installed them all and they settled very quickly into their new home. We were advised to keep them in their run for three days but after a day an adventurous hen led the great escape and we let them have their freedom. They were all very good and came back happily to roost at night. So far so good…..

I quickly discovered that having your first chickens has many similarities to having a first baby. Okay, it's nothing like as painful and at least marginally less expensive but the world suddenly becomes full of experts, all with conflicting advice. 'Don't put hay in the nest boxes,' a book would say sternly, 'it may contain harmful spores.' 'Hay is the best thing for nest boxes,' stated a friend with masses of healthy chickens, 'they don't like straw.' 'Give them corn.' 'Give them layers pellets.' 'Worm regularly.' 'Don't worm.' For every bit of advice gleaned, a new contrary piece of information would counteract it. Soon our domestic conversation revolved around the health and well-being of our new flock, who went about their business quite happily, without much if any help from us.

Then my husband decided to make some improvements to the coop. The first of these was to raise the chicken house about eighteen inches above the ground on wooden posts. The chickens looked on anxiously as he dismantled their new house and nailed the floor to the posts. There wasn't time or timber to make ramps, so he constructed a picturesque pile of logs at each pop-hole to enable them to climb up. A few of the hens watched this with interest clucking to each other, just like a group of housewives watching a workman. If they'd had hands, they would have been on their hips: 'Ooh look. What's he doing that for?'

'Tut, tut, tut. It'll never work you know.'

Once it was finished though, this little group climbed up the logs, checked it all out and come bedtime were happily ensconced on their perches.

That evening I noticed my husband was taking a long time shutting up the chickens and went out to

21

see what was happening. I found him chasing chickens all over the garden. Most of them (including all the cockerels of course) had been completely unable to work out how to get into their house. Trying not to laugh and catch chickens at the same time wasn't easy. However, I thought by the following night, once they had climbed out from their lofty house, they would have grasped the new procedure. It was dark when I got home from work but the garden appeared quiet. I opened the back door and nearly fell over a group of chickens, huddled on the doormat. It took a week before the last one got the hang of it.

It's been interesting to observe how male and female chickens follow similar patterns to their human counterparts. The girls are productive and hard working: laying eggs, trying to hatch them and looking for food. The males strut around, posing, fighting and making a huge amount of noise but achieving very little, apart from bothering the females. Any parent wanting an object lesson for a teenage daughter in male sexuality could do worse than encouraging a spot of chicken watching. My husband thought one of our hens had actually died from the cockerel's amorous attentions, but after a minute of lying prone, she got up and shook herself, whereupon he immediately resumed where he'd left off. Mind you, we've also seen hens lead the cockerel on, only to change their minds and run away....

We've been pleasantly surprised to find our chickens are more intelligent and individual than we imagined. They are deeply curious and the braver ones (oddly, usually the hens) love exploring. It's taken a while but some of them have now mustered the courage to join us in the conservatory, which opens on to the garden. With around two acres to play in, it's hard to see why they would want to come into the house but looking at them, I can see a certain defiance in their beady eyes. They come in because they can and I think they dare each other. Obviously this isn't something to be encouraged.

It's interesting to see how the flock follows a structured routine. This mainly revolves around eating, sleeping and preening, but each activity has its own allocated time in the day. I've noticed that their timetable is quite similar to our pony and imagine it is based on temperature and light but I still find it impressive that the animals are so organised.

Coming home from work on a warm afternoon, I've found the pony sleeping soundly in the shade and the chickens happily snoozing under the trees. Hot and tired I've gone indoors, wondering just who is the superior species." *[Anne also writes about her Black Rocks - see page 115].*

## ANCONA

The Ancona hen, as the name suggests, originated in Italy. Both the cock and hen are similar in colour – a mottled black and white and they tend to have elongated bodies. The single comb on the female tends to flop over on one side. The hens lay white eggs and are very similar to Leghorns. Anconas love foraging and digging in bushes and among plants so look out if they are running free in your garden. They are also good flyers, being sprightly and lightweight. The feathers on Ancona hens are renewed each year with larger white spots after the moult so older Anconas will look whiter, rather like grey horses which become whiter with age. Anconas are available as large fowl or bantams and are classed as soft-feathered and light.

*Angela Sturt from Shrewton, Wiltshire writes*:

"I remember an Ancona bantam I had a few years ago. She was a great character and we loved her - she had the weirdest ideas on the best places for egg laying - her best efforts were in the garage in my bicycle basket and one day when the back door was open she strolled into the utility room and took up residence in the Jack Russell's box and settled down to lay in there. Unfortunately she was disturbed by the Jack Russell or she would have succeeded I am sure."

## APPENZELLER SPITZHAUBEN

This is a crested breed from Switzerland recently imported into Britain. Appenzellers come in three colours: silver-spangled, gold-spangled or black. They are particularly attractive and this is why I am including this rare breed. The cocks look magnificent with their beautiful tail feathers and small head crests. This is a light soft-feathered breed and I have heard that they can be quite flighty, contrary to the following comment. The hens lay white eggs.

*Mrs Kramer from Southern Alabama, USA writes*:

"I find that these are very personable and tame chickens. I had a hen for years that just adored my husband. Every time he went near her she would fly up and perch on his shoulder. He was not especially fond of this behaviour so he usually avoided her."

*Frances Ockford from Pocklington, Yorkshire writes*:

"Appenzellers are The Dalmatians of the poultry world, and what characters and active birds these were. I started off with a silver pair, Siegfried and Heidi. They produced several batches of chicks, that ran before they could walk and while the Brahma chicks were still deciding to get on to their legs after hatching, the Appenzellers were up and off!! Great fun but sadly there are not many around now, and they have been taken over by the Rare Breed Poultry Society."

## ARAUCANA

Araucanas were bred by the Indians from the Arauca Province of Northern Chile, South America, who refused to let the Spanish conquerors crossbreed their hens. They are the only hens in the world to lay turquoise eggs (colours vary between green, olive and blue) but no one knows quite why they do. Araucanas are crested and have faces covered with thick muffling. They have pea combs with an often irregular slightly twisted shape. They come in many colours including lavender, blue, silver, black and white. There is also a Rumpless variation of the breed which, as the name suggests, does not have a tail but

26

is favoured because it lays a large egg in relation to its body size. In fact in America the standard Araucanas are Rumpless. The breed has only become popular relatively recently. The Araucana can be successfully crossed with other breeds and the eggs will still be blue or green, due to a dominant gene – crossing with white egg layers tends to result in blue eggs, while crossing with brown egg layers tends to result in khaki green eggs. Araucanas are quite flighty and like to roam and so may not be ideal for small gardens. They are available as large fowl or bantams and are a light soft-feathered breed. The autosexing breed, Cream Legbars, have been developed using Araucanas crossed with Leghorns. (These are bred so that female and male chicks can be distinguished by colour).

*David Penfold from Norfolk writes:*

"Last summer I received an e-mail from one of the girls in the office - 'Chicken Going Spare'; that is how Hannah, an Araucana bantam, entered my life.

After a couple of weeks' quarantine, I thought that it was high time that Hannah joined the other three hens in their project of landscaping my garden. The ark door was opened and I waited to see what happened next. The date was the Fourth of July, I should have remembered that Hannah was of American descent!

For an hour or so the chooks did what chooks do relatively peacefully so I carried on with my chores, checking on the garden at regular intervals. After one such check there were only three heads not four, no Hannah! Several circuits of the garden confirmed that I might not know where she was, but I knew where she wasn't.

The neighbours had their peaceful Sunday interrupted whilst gardens were searched for errant chickens, all to no avail.

A five acre smallholding backs onto my garden and that too was fruitlessly searched. I returned home dejectedly.

Shortly afterwards I looked into the garden and who should be strutting about? You've guessed it, but by the time I had got there the lady had vanished again! Half an hour later the telephone rang, it was my smallholding neighbours with news of Hannah's capture.

Shortly afterwards box containing a somewhat disgruntled chicken was passed over the fence. She had tunnelled under the fence.

Was it my fancy or did I hear strains of Elmer Bernstein's theme as I put Hannah back into the 'cooler'?

My only worry now is that she will learn how to ride a motorbike…..!"

*Juliette Atkinson from Norfolk writes*:

"Having managed to keep hens through two winters, the purchase of two young pullets to keep everyone fit and healthy seemed a good idea. Having read a few articles about breeds, the Lavender Araucana seemed ideal. A smallish hen with a little top knot of feathers and reportedly quite gentle and friendly. After some searching I found a wonderful farm where they bred them and two were duly ordered. From the moment they arrived home they behaved differently from my other hens. The hen house was subdivided to protect them and they had their own private run but even after a couple of weeks, they were no nearer to getting used to me or allowing me near them. All my other ladies will come close to get titbits and, with reluctance, they can be picked up – although I have to say I don't find chickens particularly cuddly.

The time came for them to start integrating with the rest of the flock – of course there was the usual amount of organising into pecking order, but the two new birds were such fast runners – it felt more like owning two young pheasants. The first evening at dusk the Araucanas were missing. The Orpingtons had roosted in trees when they were young, so I searched the tall laurel at the side of the run and yes, there they were and very high up too. The laurel isn't suitable for climbing, it has not got big enough branches and it's too dense for a ladder. I thought of the net I used for the pond, it has a long handle with a large hooped net on the top. Much to my surprise, when the net got near to the first hen, instead of falling into it, she stood on the hoop and continued to roost. Gently I lowered the net and popped her in the hen house. The second hen did exactly the same and so my routine of 'the chicken lift' started. After about a month of this interesting night-time entertainment, I decided to build a covered run for them so they would learn to go in without roosting. After a month or so, they were let out and it was partially successful with the odd bout of forgetfulness on the part of the Araucanas.

As winter came sadly one of the Araucanas, the tamer if either were tame at all, suddenly died – a friend has told me that chickens are either alive or dead and that there is no in between. Vets often seem to dose hens with antibiotics but not always with much success. This left my one rather lonely Araucana running around the garden like an Olympic athlete. She does follow the others around, but, she is bottom of the pecking order, she has taken to bullying everything else that's smaller than her – doves, ducks, pigeons and even my cat.

She doesn't appear to have a maternal feather on her – her egg laying is something else – it takes place on the run! She refuses to use a nesting box but prefers the hard bricks of my patio which are quite a challenge for an egg shell. Two out of every three days are spent searching for the elusive blue egg. My dog is delighted by the whole affair as we have a tradition that broken or cracked eggs are 'Digby eggs' and he now has a regular supply of scramble to look forward to. The most interesting egg laying took place on a wall – one moment she was standing eyeing up the wild bird table and the next she'd moved off leaving an egg standing on its end on the wall held in place by a bit of dropping. Oh for a camera at the right time, it doesn't sound very plausible, does it?

Well, I now have the full range of egg colours in my kitchen and a very entertaining if rather wild bird to watch as she careers around. *[Juliette also has Cochins, Welsummers, Buff Orpingtons and a Jersey Giant - see page 42 and 50]* Perhaps not all Araucana hens behave like this, but she has made me appreciate the placid natures of my other larger ladies and any future purchases will be more in the Buff Orpington line."

*Here is an account of a more placid and much appreciated Araucana.*

**Emma Elliot from the Isle of Lewis, Western Isles, Scotland writes:**

"I bid for six Lavender Araucana eggs on eBay. They arrived and amidst pleasant surprise at just how blue they really were, we popped the eggs into the incubator and 21 days later out hatched three very small, fluffy chicks. I was delighted to see that the chicks really were lavender coloured, well, more pale lilac than lavender. They grew quickly and it soon became apparent that we had reared two cockerels and a hen, which we now refer to as Ms Araucana.

The cockerels are rather prehistoric-looking birds, very upright with legs so dark grey they could almost be black and their toes are tipped with sharp talons. Their combs and faces are livid red with bright, beady eyes that monitor your every move. However, Ms Araucana is quite different. True, she still has dark legs and long, sharp talons but everything else about her is quite different and much softer.

She's a shorter, plumper bird and whilst her brothers have become darker with age, Ms Araucana's plumage has lightened to a beautiful, luminous, very pale grey. For all her beauty, Ms Araucana is the ultimate bearded lady. She sports a fine mass of feathers around her face that obscures her wattles to such a degree that I can honestly say I've never seen them. Of all my chickens, Ms Arauacana will forever hold a special place in my heart. She's usually the first to greet you at the fence, racing over from wherever she's pecking, head down, back flattened and her legs sprinting in a manner that always reminds me of the Road Runner. She's the one that follows you around the chicken run, right on your heels so you have to be careful not to tread on her and, if you are quiet and gentle enough, she will even oblige you with a cuddle in order that you might feel how soft her feathers really are!  All this I realise is merely cupboard love, for she is the greediest of my chickens and only behaves in this way in the hope that you might throw her some grain or present her lovingly with a bowl of kitchen scraps, but I don't mind being used in such a way for she is my one and only Ms Araucana."

*The author writes:*

"We have an Araucana cross – a black hen, Molly, with a little hat and a very elegant stance. She roamed a bit too far recently out of our field and on to the public footpath. It was there that a dog encountered her, giving chase up the path and on to a back road – the owner of the dog lost sight of them for a few minutes and when she had managed to bring her dog back to heel our hen had disappeared, leaving a bunch of feathers in various places.  We went out to search the area that evening and the next morning to no avail. Fearing the inevitable we gave up hope of seeing her again. However later in the morning I went out on my bike down the road branching off the back road. Who should I meet but Molly walking sedately along the road, but quickly disappearing into the bushes as I approached and a car came from the opposite direction. I rushed home, collected my sons and we managed to catch her and bring her safely home. She was absolutely fine and promptly went off to lay an egg – my nine year old son said it was a miracle and gave her a kiss and a cuddle.

We also have one pure lavender Araucana who as a result of losing her partner is a real loner. She is totally free range but when one of our Black Rocks approaches she squats down and allows herself to be pecked on the neck. Seeing her at the mercy of this large hen, I can't say I find my Black Rocks that endearing."

## BARNEVELDER

This breed derives its name from the town where it was developed, Barneveld in Holland. Most farmers in the surrounding area of Barneveld were keeping poultry as early as the 12th century. Around 1850 the poultry there were crossed with imported stock such as Cochins, Malays, Brahmas and Langshans and the value of selection for utility was discovered – egg production improved substantially and brown eggs were the preferred colour. The eventual result at the turn of the century was the Barnevelder. The inhabitants of Barneveld always claimed that their chickens laid 313 eggs – being a religious community with no work being done on Sundays, that was 365 days minus 52 Sundays. However this may be a little optimistic – egg production is more likely to be about 200 eggs a year. Barnevelders, as might be expected, are the most popular dual purpose breed in Holland – the climate there is often cold, windy and damp. This made Barnevelders a thrifty and hardy breed and very suitable for the similar variable climate in Britain. Barnevelders were imported into Britain in the early 1900s. The hens nowadays are good layers of dark brown eggs – Maranses were used to improve the dark brown colour of the eggs. Colour variations in the birds are black, double-laced (black with beetle green sheen), partridge and silver. This is a heavy soft-feathered breed and the bantams are replicas of their large fowl counterparts.

Back in Holland Barnevelder hens have certainly helped the development of their native town, Barneveld, where poultry, eggs and associated products are still a major source of income in the area. The Dutch Poultry Museum is based there and it is also the home of the International Barneveld College, an educational poultry institute.

*Emma Everett from Farnham, Surrey writes:*

"My Barnevelder hen, Tulip, became legendary at home due to her survival techniques. When all the other hens who lived with her were eaten by a fox she was the only remaining hen.

Then in the hurricane of 1987 the roof flew off the chicken hutch and she was found a day later crouching in a corner of the broken hutch so she came on the 'school run' that day and then lived in the house and then the stable for a couple of days.

Her next escape came when a puppy got into her hutch and bit a chunk out of her back. She was rushed to the vet and stitched up. She went on living for a further five years and Tulip continued to lay eggs until she died (even though they were a slightly funny shape on occasions). She was the loveliest pet and became a favourite hen."

## BELGIAN BEARDED BANTAMS

Three varieties are standardised in Britain: Barbu D'Uccle (Bearded Uccle) is, as the name suggests, heavily feathered around the neck with feathered feet. It has a single comb and comes in many colour variations including black-mottled, lavender, porcelaine, millefleur and laced-blue. The amazing choice of colours in these bantams is probably unrivalled in any other breed. They lay small cream eggs. Barbu D'Anvers (Bearded Antwerp) differs from the Barbu d'Uccle in that it has clean legs, a rose comb and in the males the wings are carried very low, almost vertically. Barbu De Watermael (Bearded Watermael) is crested and clean-legged, small and perky. All three remind one of a human wearing an overcoat with the collar turned up. These are one of the oldest true bantam breeds. A Dutch painting from the 17th century by a certain Albert Cuyp reveals a small hen with similar markings to a quail-coloured Barbu D'Anvers.

*Ann Lloyd from Manchester writes:*

"I have kept and shown Belgian Bantams for some years. I don't have a cockerel because my neighbours are so close so when I get a broody hen I go to my local community farm for fertile eggs and then take the birds back to them when they are pullets. A couple of years ago I had an elderly bantam called Deuteronomy who was a Barbu D'Anvers. She was a fantastic broody and hatched many chicks over the years. The last time she was broody I went to the farm for some eggs for her (I hate to waste a broody hen) and they had none, only one duck egg, so Deuteronomy sat on her egg and eventually hatched a cute little duckling which she fussed over in her usual manner. She should have realised that something was amiss when it didn't want to scratch in the dust with her!

I was in the kitchen one morning when I heard her screaming in a total panic. I rushed out thinking our urban fox was hoping for breakfast to find the duckling swimming merrily round in the pond while poor Deuteronomy rushed round the edge in a terrible state; to add insult to injury the duckling turned out to be a Muscovy duck and was very soon much bigger than Mum. It tried to get under her wing to brood and she ended up sitting on its back.

We had some laughs while we had it but I was glad to see it go as it nearly filled my tiny garden. I think Deuteronomy was glad to see the back of it as well. I love to sit and watch my girls. They give me such pleasure and are very intelligent."

*Ann Lloyd also writes:*

"I hand-reared a chick once from one day old until she was relegated to the garden when her poos got too big to cope with ! I used to take her shopping in my pocket on the bus and she slept in a woollen blanket in a cardboard box by my bed. I had a friend who had a beard and she used to love to snuggle under it – such a funny sight to see her little head pop out from under his beard. She followed me all over the place but had a struggle getting upstairs. She would cheep madly when tired and I would pop her in my pocket for a snooze. She went on to rear a few of her own chicks and was called Lucky."

*Angela Sturt from Wiltshire writes about her very friendly Barbu D'Uccle:*

"One day in the summer I had just given my hens their corn and my husband and I sat down in the garden with a cup of tea to watch them all. I put the bucket of corn beside me on the ground. This little Barbu D'Uccle came up to us, hopped into the bucket and settled down and laid her egg there! Very sweet and confiding, I thought."

## BRAHMA

The Brahma is a very old breed supposedly from India and early pictures show that it was very similar to the Cochin from China. The name Brahma is taken from the river Brahmaputra in India. However, it is now generally agreed that the Brahma was created in America from Shanghais or Cochins imported from China in the 1800s and crossed with Grey Chittagongs (Malay type birds from India). It is known that a crate of nine Brahmas was sent to Queen Victoria in 1852 from the American breeder Burnham and thus the breed was introduced to Britain. Brahmas have distinctive feathered legs and feet and a pea comb. They come in a variety of types and colours including dark, buff, light, birchen and dark Columbian. They are a heavy, soft-feathered breed and lay tinted eggs.

Brahmas are very large – they have a sort of majestic massiveness and have been variously described as 'noble and commanding', 'intelligent looking', 'with a neck well proportioned and finely curved as in a spirited horse'. Buff Brahmas are probably the most popular variety. Brahmas can weigh from 5kg (11lb) to 6kg (13lb) so are not ideal for small children. They do need space but, because they don't fly, are easy to keep in a run. They have been used in the creation of many new breeds and in developing new colours in existing ones.

*Fifteen year old Liam Kelleher from Birmingham writes:*

"I have various different breeds of hens including Brahmas, Silkies, Andalusians and a cross breed bantam. I am writing to you about my Brahmas – I have 16 and they are all my favourites – their temperament is very docile, they are clumsy and not aggressive in any way. They get very cheeky at times – when I let them out of their pen for the first time they stayed close, but gradually they went further and further away and one hen which has just started laying doesn't use her nest box. She will lay her egg anywhere. Sometimes she will even go up onto her roost and try and lay it up there but I soon get her down and put her in the nest box."

## COCHIN

The Cochin originally came from China in the 1850s where it was known as the Shanghai. It originally had clean legs and became very popular in this country owing to its size and laying powers. However exhibition breeders turned the Cochin into a 'bag of feathers' and it eventually lost its good name. Now similar to the Brahma with feathered legs and feet, it is a heavy soft-feathered breed and lays tinted eggs. There are no miniatures of this bird but Pekin bantams are a similar small version.

*Juliette Atkinson from Norfolk writes*:

"My first birds were Cochins because of their quaint fluffy legs but a couple of Welsummers, Buff Orpingtons and a rather lovely Jersey Giant soon followed.

The hens free range around the garden, eating their way through delphiniums and lupins en-route to the orchard.

Last year, a mallard duck hatched a brood of ducklings and left two eggs in the nest when she moved off. As they were still warm, a neighbour challenged my broody Cochin hen to hatch them. Much to everyone's surprise one of the eggs did hatch and my hen didn't seem at all surprised to have a duckling instead of a chick. We protected the pair from the not entirely kind attentions of the other hens and some magpies until the duckling had grown to a reasonable size. The duckling showed no signs of wanting to play in water or to be aware that she wasn't a chicken, trundling into the hen house each night to roost, albeit on the floor not on the perch! We tried to entice her to swim in a paddling pool, in fact we spent hours inflating the wretched thing only to have her turn her bill up at it. We needn't have worried, eventually she found our pond and other young ducks and now resides in the garden with her mate and no doubt more ducklings will soon be on the way."

## CROAD LANGSHAN

Langshans were first imported into Britain by Major Croad from China where they are said to have originated in the Monasteries. Most common in black

43

with a beautiful green tinge, there is also a rare white variety. They both have a single comb and lightly feathered legs and feet. Langshans lay deep brown eggs. There is also a Modern Langshan breed which has been developed along different lines.

*Eris from Sussex writes:*

"The Croad Langshan as well as being a wonderful looking bird has a very deep resonant crow, that many people at shows always comment on as being a 'lovely sound'. Certainly something that can't often be said for most bantam breeds."

*Clare Curtis from Cheshire writes :*

"We started keeping poultry in 1998 with half a dozen Warrens and swiftly expanded our small flock to include firstly Cuckoo Marans then a few Sussex. The flock remained quite mixed until recently when our resident cock died and we decided to choose a pure breed to keep and hopefully breed from.

Choosing a breed was quite a challenge. We were keen to keep large fowl for the eggs but also like striking-looking birds. The Croad Langshans were appealing and we contacted the breed club to source a trio.

Wallace and his two Croad females arrived in December 2004 and quickly settled in. It wasn't long before I was incubating my first eggs and hatching chicks. Disaster struck at Easter when we lost Wallace, but not before he had sired ten young pullets and a solitary handsome male, Wallace Junior.

Croad Langshans are content and friendly birds who are always keen to know what is going on. They rush out on to the drive when they hear anyone arriving to see who it is, and regularly follow me down the path until they find something more interesting that takes their attention.

The Croads lay beautiful large plum-coloured eggs. They make a good job of keeping the lawn moss free and are not too destructive in the flower borders. It's lovely to have them roaming around the garden and they are a real talking point with visitors. Watching them is a constant delight.

Wallace Junior is a gentle giant, not yet fully grown and with only the suggestion of what hopefully will be a magnificent tail, he already has the respect of the mature hens in the flock. His large dark intelligent eyes watch while he feeds from the hand and picks seeds daintily from offered fingers. Comfortable with his surroundings he struts around the garden, master of all he surveys. One moment he is running swiftly to check on the hen that has just laid, and the next leading a group into the kitchen in search of sultana treats.

A while later he stands tall and alert before a shrill alarm call and commotion send him dashing through the gate to the back garden. A sparrow hawk flies low over the garden and just as quickly leaves. Upright, watching, still, quiet, Wallace mutters to the flock and walks away."

## DORKING

It is thought that the Dorking is one of the oldest domesticated fowl, possibly introduced into Britain by the Romans, and was described by Pliny in his Natural History. The five toes are a distinctive feature of the Dorking. It is a heavy, soft-feathered breed laying tinted eggs. In the female, the single comb flops over to one side. Dorkings are large but have short legs. Colours vary from cuckoo to red, silver grey and white. This breed is on the Rare Breeds Survival Trust list. However the breed has been used in autosexing to produce the Dorbar.

*Frances Ockford from Pocklington, Yorkshire writes:*

"A good Dorking is a joy to behold, and characteristically boat shaped. I love the silver greys – they are slow to mature and can be quite heavy. The combs come in a variety of shapes and sizes too, which makes the breed interesting. The silver grey hens have a very delicate shading of grey pencilled feathers and the contrasting salmon breast and unusual five toes. Dorkings are not the easiest birds to rear; they do not do well in damp conditions. The hens seem to lay well at the beginning of the year and tend to go broody too. It became a bit of a joke with the members of the Dorking Club whenever we were asked how our birds were doing, and we optimistically replied laying well, maturing etc. The next day one would be found dead!!!"

## DUTCH BANTAM

The Dutch Bantam originated in Holland but wasn't introduced to Britain until the 1960s. Available in a multitude of colours, they are popular both as pets and exhibition birds. The Dutch Bantam is an alert, active bird with an upright jaunty appearance. Wings are carried low and although ear lobes are white, they lay tinted eggs.

*Jennifer Denny from Ashford, Kent writes*:

"We had chickens years ago and gradually lost them to foxes, but, after giving up keeping horses due to my age, I decided to try again. Using electric poultry netting which has been successful at keeping out foxes (so far) for two years I had bred three charming tiny Dutch Partridge bantams. I kept them in a run for quite a while so, before I put them in a large electrified pen, I decided to clip their wings (one wing each in the approved manner.) Where should I attempt this? They get hysterical quite easily – our small shower room seemed a good idea so I got them into a small box and carried it up to the room. The clipping was successful but I forgot to shut the loo lid – two ended up there and one in the basin – husband and spaniel wondered what on earth was happening! Anyway all was well – they love their large pen – respect the fence – as do the foxes – and eat out of my hand now."

# FAYOUMI

This is a rare Egyptian breed from the district of Fayoum (meaning water) south of Cairo. Fayoumis have been raised along the Nile since early times existing as free ranger scavengers. They were introduced into Britain in 1984 by the Domestic Fowl Trust. Fayoumis are hardy, quick to mature and good fliers so not ideal for small gardens. They are very attractive and can be silver or gold-pencilled. The hens lay white eggs. No other breed matures as quickly as the Fayoumi – pullets may start to lay small eggs at four months and the cockerels may start to crow at rather an unbelievable six weeks old! Both hens and cockerels are VERY flighty......like bullets! They're also very attractive and naturally very disease-resistant. The cockerels are striking-looking birds when their sickle feathers are fully formed and they have jet black, piercing eyes. Fayoumis are not a beginner's bird and not ideal for small gardens.

*Eris from Sussex writes:*

"Some breeds of hens are designed for, and far better off, being permitted to live the most natural life possible. They truly dislike living in the confines of small coops. The ones that spring to mind are breeds like the Egyptian Fayoumi. These breeds take to living up trees like a duck takes to water. Give them a nice cosy house and it frequently will be spurned for the

49

nearest bush or tree as a preferable roosting place. The house is a convenient laying place but no more than that. Not that they won't live the life of a domestic fowl, they will of course. However there is always a certain something in their attitude that makes you think that they are only really doing it to accommodate you, not actually out of preference."

## JERSEY GIANT

Jersey Giants are large fowl originating in New Jersey in America around 1880. The breed became known as 'Giant' because specimens were recorded weighing up to 5.90kg (13lb). The Jersey Giant is made up from breeds which include the black Java, dark Brahma, black Langshan and Indian Game. Although exceptionally heavy, Jersey Giants are very adaptable to free range conditions, making excellent foragers and are layers of large eggs. Typically Jersey Giants are black but white and more rarely blue are also recognised colours.

*Juliette Atkinson from Norfolk writes:*

"Like my lone Araucana, the Jersey Giant roams the garden as my only black hen. An article somewhere on the breed said that nothing was as striking as a flock of black Jersey Giants roaming over fresh green grass, and it's true that her wonderful black plumage which shines blue and green in the sunlight is very striking. As well as the black plumage, she has dark brown eyes with a rather knowing expression about them. My mother has nicknamed her 'the Pirate' which seems to suit her. Along with my Buff Orpingtons and Cochins she particularly seems to enjoy a morning slot of television; the hens like to come to the French windows that look into my kitchen and watch while we're eating breakfast, tapping on the glass as if trying to change channels – reality TV for hens!

Apart from her great plumage, her habit of laying an egg every other day all through the winter when everyone else is off lay is very much appreciated. I'm not sure if this is anything to do with her breed, or just luck. It's great being able to tell which hen laid which egg and hers are lovely creamy coloured eggs with brown speckles.

Jersey Giants are energetic foragers and when I purchased them, she and her sister, now unfortunately departed, were very agile and adventurous. This enthusiasm for acrobatics eventually caused a damaged spine in the sister for which there was no remedy. As the hens have freedom all over our garden, they make full use of walls and steps and ditches to keep fit. I often have a row of hens standing like parachutists on the 3 foot wall outside my kitchen window waiting to jump off into the long grass and daffodils below – they could walk down the steps but I suppose it wouldn't be so much fun. Although the Jersey Giant is a large hen, she is definitely more compact and traditional in shape than the Orpingtons who were bred for size and fluffiness.

A friend in the village thinks I'm mad – he changes his Marans hens every couple of years to keep egg yields high, whereas my pet hens will live out their natural lives in the garden. I haven't bought any young pullets this year, one reason is indecision – my husband loves the Orpingtons for their amber colour and their tutu-like rump feathers, but in books and magazines I read articles about all the other breeds and there are so many to choose from. Therefore I think I can safely say that when next Spring comes, I'll be putting in an order for at least another pair of Jersey Giants."

## LAKENVELDER

It is unclear whether this breed originated in the Netherlands or Germany. The Dutch claim the Lakenvelder was named after the village of Lakenvelt. Others think that the name came from Lakenvel, meaning shadow on a sheet. Others say the breed was named after Lakenvelder cattle which have a black head and tail and white over the rest of their body. It is also generally believed that the breed originated in the Westphalian area of Germany.

Lakenvelders are striking with their white feathered bodies contrasting with black neck and tail feathers. This colour marking is called belted. They have longish bodies. They lay white eggs, are non-sitters and flighty, not liking to be cooped up.

*Eris from Sussex writes*:

"Lakenvelders are certainly very beautiful, and to produce a well marked one is no easy task. However they do seem to be very alert to any passing potential predator or unusual activity, and will set all my other birds off with a cacophony of clucking and squawking. But if you aren't worried by the noise their beauty and lovely white eggs more than make up for their rather frequent tantrums."

## LEGHORN

A very popular light breed which originated from the Port of Leghorn in Italy and was imported into Britain in the late 1800s, with white first and then brown Leghorns. Leghorns have had the longest life of any of the productive breeds ever introduced. It was a light bird originally and there is evidence from old pictures that this type of bird with a flop-over comb in the female was to be found in many countries of Europe. Old breeds such as the Belgian Brakel, Pheasant Fowls and the Scots Grey had similar features such as white ear lobes, flop-over combs and laid white eggs. It is possible therefore that this Mediterranean type was the original fowl of Europe and that the heavier type of Leghorn evident today was due to crossing Malays, Cochins and Minorcas. Prolific layers of white eggs, Leghorns are a light, soft-feathered breed and non-sitters. There are now other colour variations available such as black, barred, buff, cuckoo, mottled and partridge, and bantams are miniatures of their large fowl counterparts.

### *Mrs Ryder from Bristol writes*:

"We had two white leghorns, thin, flighty creatures who laid huge white eggs. One of them became very tame. I spent my boarding school holidays all day with the hens, taming them. I even taught them tricks like flying onto my arms or shoulders at an order. The favourite, La Favorita, discovered a secret way out of the field and into our garden. Her joy was for someone to take a spade and start digging a bed. She ate the worms and crawlies in huge numbers, resulting in huge flavoursome eggs. One summer's day my father, mother, young brother and I were enjoying tea on a blanket on the lawn. A robin was in attendance and soon La Favorita joined us to partake of the bits of bread and crusts from our sandwiches. All was peace and happiness. But as so often happens our cat decided to come and spoil things. The grass at the edge of the lawn was deep. The cat came creeping through it on low legs after the robin who was totally unaware of its danger. But then – tall thin elegant Leghorn – could see the cat and was aware of the robin's danger. She made a sudden lunge at the robin who flew up just as the cat sprang. La Favorita obviously saved her pal's life."

*Shirley West from Wiltshire writes:*

"What is it about folk who move to the country and have the urge to keep chickens?

It always seems like 'a good idea at the time'! So being completely clueless about the upkeep of chickens we become the proud owners of three black leghorns, and fine specimens they are too! People who are in 'the know' tell you that chickens are a bit dim, a bit unkind we thought! We acquired one of those Arks to house them in which are pretty good as they can be moved around the garden so keeping the ground in some sort of good order (that is until the said chickens start digging for victory).

After a couple of weeks we moved the Ark a couple of feet to the right. That evening at sun-set (chickens do have a good body clock) we waited for them to retire to bed. We waited and waited. We were ready for bed ourselves and eventually we thought they must have gone up so went to lock them in for the night (this is a must to keep them safe from predators who fancy some chicken for their supper) but no chickens! We searched the grounds to no avail; had they managed to tunnel their way out and were they now surfacing somewhere in France? At this point I must point out that behind the Ark is a Leylandii hedge roughly 20ft high. My husband and I and my daughter were all out armed with torches searching through the hedge and there they were fast asleep. We had a devil of a job retrieving them and they were not too happy either being pulled out by their legs!

Another time we had retired to bed and were fast asleep when I suddenly awoke with a start. We had forgotten to lock them in. I woke my husband who immediately jumped out of bed and rushed outside to lock them up; it was two o'clock in the morning and he was stark naked!

After a while the chickens really made themselves at home, we even had names for them. They were so at home that one morning I found two of them in the kitchen helping themselves to the cat food and being observed by one of my four cats, who incidentally, takes eating her food very seriously. It happens to be the mainstay of her life and shock horrors! - it was her bowl.

Only last week I was on the phone when I heard such a scuffle going on, I thought I was being burgled. With phone still attached to my ear I braved it into the sitting room only to find one of my darling chickens perched on my sofa being observed by three of my cats who were probably thinking, 'How dare these birds of the feathered variety which we cannot catch, play with or eat, enter our domain?' While still on the phone I managed to open the window and shoo it out only to find she had left me a 'present' on my rug. I think the chap I was talking to found me quite mad. This may not have held too well with said insurance claim!

They are still not satisfied with all our ground and are often seen trotting down the lane, probably having a good gossip and putting the world to rights, just like a Walt Disney film. Fortunately for us it is usually a happy ending."

*Ivan Mears from Milton Keynes, Buckinghamshire writes:*

"I have flirted with keeping Leghorns on and off most of my life and although I've enjoyed keeping other breeds the Leghorn is now my firm favourite. The colour range is immense, but the Exchequer, Blue Red, Silver Duckwing and Black are my favourite colours. They seem to be the precocious fowl of the yard, with high scarlet headgear and yellow legs foraging energetically. They seem to be saying, 'Don't look at the others, look at Me.' They are white egg layers and lay really well. A much larger egg is laid in the second year. They are quick to mature so cocks are more readily identifiable. I hope this will encourage people to try this cheeky breed and encourage breeding them to ensure the genetic pool continues."

## MARANS

English ships sailing into Marans in France, near La Rochelle, in the 1800s used to carry hens and fighting cocks. These were exchanged with fresh hens from Marans and the region became the birthplace of a particular breed of poultry, originally called the Marandaise, later to become the Marans. Around 1880 two brothers, poultry merchants from London, were responsible for spreading knowledge of the Marans hens. One of them was a wholesaler of white Russian eggs (Russia was at this time an important poultry producing country). The other brother, whose ships docked at Marans, had the idea of competing with the white Russian egg trade by selling the dark brown eggs of Marans hens which were bigger and fresher. Thus the eggs soon became popular in the London markets. Maranses were crossed with Brahmas and

Langshans in order to make the eggs browner – Brahmas were used for their egg laying abilities and the Langshans for the dark brown colour of their eggs. Maranses weren't actually introduced to Britain until 1929. They are a heavy breed and are the one breed where it is relatively easy to distinguish male and female chicks – males have a white spot on the top of their heads while females have a darker one. They lay very large deep brown eggs and are a good choice of breed for free range as they forage well. Bantams are available as miniatures of their large fowl counterpart. The Cuckoo coloured variety is the most popular. They can look similar to the Barred Plymouth Rocks. Marans' eggs are so special that in France competitions are held on the size, shape, texture and dark colour of the eggs. The colour ranges from brown to a dark chocolate colour. Bantams are usually not that tame and not particularly keen on being touched. Hens are large and heavy. I have heard that they can be unreliable layers but worth keeping just for the colour of the eggs.

*The author writes:*

"We have two Marans bantams who started laying for the first time this year, although I wasn't getting many eggs from them. However I noticed that the less tame of the two was missing for most of the day. I followed her as she disappeared into an old garage belonging to my neighbour. I crept in early the next morning and discovered that she was surrounded by a sea of small dark brown eggs - she was trying to sit on an astounding 36 eggs. She is obviously new to the trade and didn't realise it is more normal to lay about 11 - 13 eggs and then go broody and sit!"

*Ken Pothecary from Burridge, Southampton writes*:

"My wife, Jan, myself and six other close friends had booked a long weekend in a farm cottage. The cottage was delightful and to top the welcome was a basket of fresh brown speckled eggs and an invitation to help ourselves to any more we might need from the chicken run at the bottom of the garden. The weekend was a great success. One of the other couples already kept chickens and were also smitten with these feathered friends who turned out to be grey speckled Maranses and handsome red brown Welsummers. Jan by this stage had started to turn broody and when our friends announced that they had an incubator buried in their garage and wouldn't it be a good idea to take some eggs home and hatch them out, my goose was cooked. Plans were made for me to build a chicken house and run when I got home. Arriving back with a tray of eggs which our friends took to incubate, I was set to work in the garden. I spent the next few weeks building a chicken house to a plan in my head which, when completed, I was proud of if only for its uniqueness. This was followed by the chicken run, a 12 x 6 metre concentration camp type structure designed to keep Mr Fox out which needed a 2 metre high chicken wire fence buried at least 30 cm into the ground and strands of barbed wire around the top.

Whilst all this was going on the eggs duly hatched and Jan and our friend Sheila who had the incubator duly clucked and fussed over these cute bundles of fluff. There were clearly two types distinguished by colour plus a couple of odd balls and it was agreed that Sheila would keep the Welsummers and we would have the Maranses. After a few weeks of nurturing in Sheila's garage and then with one of her more reliable hens, the day came when the chickens came home to us. We had six Marans juveniles and two odd balls, referred to as eagles, who took to their new home and admired my handiwork. A couple of weeks later after much nurturing and special care we became concerned about one of the chickens who was looking distinctly different to the others. Another couple of weeks and they were becoming reasonable sized chickens and realisation started to dawn; what we had was seven cockerels and one rather worried looking hen and dreams of harvesting fresh brown eggs fast disappearing.

This was the point when the more basic rules of country living started to come to the foreground. We had seven, young, plump, well fed cockerels who were competing over one hen, who had learnt to run fast and only had one obvious use. So with the help of my neighbour who was well practised in the art, I learned to kill, pluck and prepare birds for the table.

We gained more point of lay hens as we lost cockerels by the unromantic but more reliable method of buying them from a breeder."

*Forsham Cottage Arks write in their catalogue:*

"We had a very large Marans cockerel once that my daughter christened Gorebash. He was so tall he could walk through the potato helms and see the hen in the next row. One afternoon I watched as he strode down the row, stopped, turned his head and gave an angled one-eyed glance over the mature helms, jumped the foliage and tried to give our ginger Tom cat the benefit of his manhood. Needless to say the cat was less than impressed and legged it."

## MINORCA

The Minorca probably originated in Spain and used to be very popular since it was a prolific layer of very large white eggs. Minorcas have large white ear lobes and there are black and white versions. The hen has a large single comb which drops down over her face.

*Murray Cooper from Castleton in the Peak District writes:*

"With their long legs, elegant carriage, snow white ear lobes and large combs falling rakishly to one side Minorcas remind me of well dressed ladies attending Ascot. Certainly when free ranging in a mixed flock they are always the ones that attract admiration and the inevitable question, 'What breed of chicken are those?' Underneath this flashy appearance however is a practical and productive chicken. Being the largest of the Mediterranean breeds they produce an abundance of the largest white-shelled eggs of any breed. In addition they do not go broody (often the bane of the home egg producer) and are hardy and disease resistant. The commonest colour is a glossy jet black but they are also available in snow white and a shade of medium blue. A word of warning though - just as with people who own top of the range cars or big houses it is easy to become a chicken snob looking disdainfully at those who do not own this, the king of breeds."

## OLD ENGLISH GAME

There are two varieties of Old English Game, Carlisle and Oxford. In general these Old Game varieties were used for cock fighting probably from Roman times right up until 1849 when an Act of Parliament made cock fighting illegal. It was after this that many breeders began to exhibit Game Fowl which have been bred in a multitude of colours. They are a hard-feathered breed, and are tall and slim with long legs. Bantam versions also come in a huge variety of colours. The bantams are small and lay cream eggs but are used more as show birds than for their egg laying abilities. These game breeds are not ideal for the garden – the cocks can be vicious towards each other as the following story will verify.

*Julie Hatton from Cumbria writes:*

"It started with Boss (a Heinz 57) and Dixie 1 & 2 (the Dixie Chicks who are Maranses), collected from a champion egg man. Next stop was Cockermouth auction, but I said absolutely no cockerel. So we came back with Mr & Mrs - a pair of Old English Game bantams. Mr squared up to Boss, who soon backed down. Then he started hissing at the pigeons flying over, so he changed his name to Sid. Mrs started doing aeroplane impressions around the garden, so she became Boeing.

Dixie 2 was the first to go broody on me. Naturally, we put some eggs under her and waited. It was a miracle, just like watching our Jack Russell pups being born nearly 20 years earlier. Two hatched and they were little black bundles of fluff - OEG/Maran crosses. They grew up into Blackbird and Young Cockerel and all was rosy in the garden for about six months. Then Young Cockerel started flirting with his dad's girls, which was not on. I separated them, confining the youngsters to their run and only letting them out briefly just before roosting time.

Then our beloved Jack Russell, Stanley, had to have a stay at the vets as he was so poorly. We were allowed to collect him later that afternoon, so at about 2pm I let Blackbird and Young Cockerel out. We got back from the vets about an hour and a half later and after settling Stanley, I went to check on my chickens.

Everything seemed okay, just a bit quiet. I gave them another half hour before going out to shut them up for the night - it had been snowing and the ground was totally frozen. First stop, the youngsters' house - strange, only Blackbird. Quick, look in the main house - just Boss, Boeing and The Dixies. I found Sidney just minutes from death under a bush nearby and rushed him in to ask my hubby to end his suffering. Went back for Young Cockerel - he's dead (he must have put up quite a fight though). Sidney was only just alive, we warmed him, bathed his wounds and put him in a box overnight, expecting to find him dead the next morning. He really should have been but wasn't. More wound bathing and syringing water into his mouth and he began to look fractionally better, but it still felt hopeless. Woke up the next morning to crowing - what the ****!!!! He looked like he had gone ten rounds with Mike Tyson, his eyes were glued shut and his head was just blood, but the stupid bird was welcoming in the new day! We transferred him to a dog cage and brought one of his wives in to see him - he was ecstatic and pointed to some food for her. Lots more tlc and a couple of trips to our wonderful vet and he was well enough to go back out in two weeks - confined to his run with heating in his house, but much better than the conservatory as he could see and hear his girls! Eventually his comb fell off and he wore a black scabby skull cap for a month or so, but he really did live to tell the tale and continues to be a great husband to his wives."

## ORPINGTON

Orpington fowl were named after a village in Kent where William Cook first bred them in the late 1800s. Langshans, Minorcas and Plymouth Rocks were involved in its creation and today they still look similar to the Langshan. The black variety was followed by the white and then the buff. There is now a blue variety as well. Orpingtons are compact with short legs and classified as a heavy soft-feathered breed. Bantams are also available in this breed and are very popular as they are docile and good with children. The Queen Mother used to keep large fowl Buff Orpingtons. The Black Orpington was re-introduced to this country from Australia in the 20s and called the Australorp. A later introduction was the Jubilee Orpington, which is rarely seen but has recently been added to the breeds at the Domestic Fowl Trust. Orpingtons are large, heavy and rather broad with an abundance of feathers which makes them look even bigger. They do not fly because of their weight so are easily kept within the garden. They lay well and their eggs are light brown – however the eggs are smaller than you would expect when you look at the size of the hens.

*Christine Skidmore from Pembrokeshire writes:*

"A visit to a pets' corner in a child's amusement farm resulted in our family buying three hens as pets. One was always much bigger and more boisterous than the rest and rapidly turned out to be Rocky, our black Orpington rooster, who is a sweet natured, gentle giant. Rocky disgraced himself one sunny day, when there was a birthday tea outside in the garden. Mother-in-law from the city visited (she has no love of hens at all, in fact a definite dislike)! She sat on a garden bench sipping her tea from a cup and eating a piece of football birthday cake. The rest of the family were amusing themselves by throwing titbits to the gang of gate-crashers under the table, who were welcome uninvited guests. Meanwhile Rocky was watching mother-in-law's cake and nothing else, yet nothing was coming his way. Suddenly almost as though he could sense her dislike of him, he flew up on to her lap as quick as a flash, grabbed her cake en route, causing a loud hysterical shriek. Calamity struck as mother-in-law spilt her tea and showing undisguised terror, horror and disgust, threw him off and ran for shelter into the house, amongst huge laughter from the onlookers. Rocky, however, looked decidedly pleased with himself and swelled in size as he ruffled his feathers, then wiped green icing off his beak. Unfortunately from that day onwards, he was not invited to any tea parties when mother-in-law was about but he is still a welcome guest for everyone else!"

*Sarah Ellis from Cheshire writes:*

"It had just turned dark, so I grabbed my torch and pottered out to the garden to ensure my chooks were safely away. The ex-battery girls were all roosting happily in their house, so I closed the pop hole. I went on to my two Buff Orpingtons' run, they have only been with me for three weeks so are currently in quarantine in my barn! I stepped into the run and opened the lid on the top of their house. I shone the torch in and was surprised to find just one buff sitting on the perch; very strange as they are always together! Panic began to rise as I searched the run with my beam - NOTHING!

Then as I was flicking the torch around in an increasingly manic way, I caught a glimpse of something and turned the torch upward.... I was amazed to find my Buff roosting in the rafters ten feet up! So much for large breeds being unable to fly high!!!

Happily, after being brought down (this involved a stepladder and a lot of squawking) and being put to bed with her buddy, she has taken to roosting back in her house!"

# PEKIN

The Pekin was introduced to Britain from China. In 1860 the summer palace of the Chinese Emperor at Pekin was sacked by English and French forces and some Pekin Bantams were brought home to England as plunder. The Pekin was originally thought to be a miniature of the Cochin, but in reality has no connection with it. Pekins are a genuine bantam breed and are small with feathered feet and are a wonderful tame breed for children. They are popular as they look round and cuddly. They come in a variety of colours including black, blue, buff, white, cuckoo, lavender and partridge. They don't lay particularly well and the eggs are small, being light beige. The hens go broody frequently which is fine if you want to hatch some eggs but annoying if you don't, since they are very persistent about remaining broody. Their disadvantage is that the feathered feet tend to get wet and muddy very easily. However the advantage is they won't scratch up your garden as they are hindered by their feathered feet. They will need dry conditions for perching so that their leg feathers can dry. The advantage of keeping Pekin cockerels is they crow quite softly.

*Eris from Sussex writes:*

"Pekins belie their rounded comfy appearance by actually being very busy and industrious little birds, they must surely be classed as one of the tamest of all the bantam breeds; readily becoming pets and making excellent broodies. From my experience the males are rather prone to a vast abundance of testosterone; amorously pursuing anything with feathers, moving or otherwise that catches their attention."

*Roy Taylor from Guildford, Surrey writes:*

"I hope Willie Dixon and The Rolling Stones don't mind my referring to their song 'Little Red Rooster', but I'd like to share a chicken dilemma with you. The story starts simply. Two years ago I bought two hens, 'Rocky' and 'Ginger'. Beautiful hens. Good layers. Enter fox, goodbye Rocky. Ginger needs a companion. Enter 'Amber'. After careful introduction and fisticuffs the two get along, and happy period ensues. Last summer, after a good life, Ginger pegs out.

Amber needs companion. Heart stolen by two Pekin bantam chicks, and they join the roost after careful introduction. Fisticuffs for a while from Amber even though she is roughly ten times their size and easily dominant.

As the chicks are originally from China, they get called 'Tiger Lily' and 'Lotus Blossom'. All goes well until Blossom goes mysteriously broody and will not leave nest and eggs. Tiger becomes Amber's best friend and they wander the coop like Captain Hook and Mr Smee.

As all the chickens are female, Blossom is on a lost cause with her broodiness. Decide to phone my 'chicken lady', Liz, who knows the ways of chickens and has over 100. Liz advises me to buy fertile eggs, substitute them for Blossom's own, and see what happens. How cunning is that?

Buy four fertile eggs, supposedly bantam eggs. Vast financial outlay of £1 per egg. Wait 21 days for any signs of hatching. Absolutely nothing happening. Phone Liz to complain. Go down garden to henhouse. Stone me, first shell is breaking open as I'm holding the phone to Liz! Is she a miracle worker or what!

Three of the eggs hatch. New life created in my back garden! Brilliant. One chick is black and gets called 'Pingu' after a penguin on TV. The other two are yellow and brown and simply called 'Saturday' and 'Sunday', after the days on which they were hatched.

Amber and Tiger decide to be very upset by new arrivals and hassle them at every opportunity. A normal day consists of a ritual dance, with 'Hook and Smee' chasing the mother and chicks around.

Flash forward to the present. The 'chicks' are now coming up to four months, and nature has taken a surprising course (to me anyway). Pingu has developed into a dandy little bantam hen. Saturday and Sunday, however, now tower over Blossom and Tiger and are as tall as Amber!

'Saturday' is definitely a cockerel. I know this because he is constantly trying to mate with his own foster mother, although still terrified of his little aunt. I tried telling him this is very embarrassing for me as I am a Director of Social Services and you just do not engage in this sort of behaviour with your foster mother. But it cuts no ice.

It is now well into the second week of 'Saturday' 'crowing up the day'. It began as a barely audible squeak last week, but now it's a full fledged war cry. And it's getting ever earlier as the dawn kicks in earlier. I am surrounded by neighbours' houses, and I believe the 'finger of suspicion' will point at my house very soon.

More time has passed and I now have a Brahma hen, who is huge and twice the size of the bantams; and an Araucana cross who lays green shelled eggs. The Brahma and Araucana came at the same time and we've called them Mrs Slocum (Brahma) and Miss

Brahms (Araucana). I know it's anthropomorphic but it does match their looks, with Mrs Slocum bustling about and Miss Brahms preening herself regularly. What I hadn't bargained for was the fact that the small Pekins would totally dominate hens which tower over them!"

## POLAND

The Crested Dutch or Polish were imported from Eastern Europe and in England renamed as Poland fowl. The Poland has a long history going back to the sixteenth century. It is an ornamental breed of poultry laying small white eggs. The most striking feature is its crest of feathers on top of its head. Polands are very flighty and are scared easily – this is put down to the fact that Polands find it difficult to see as the crest partially covers their eyes. For this reason it is recommended that you cut some of the feathers off round their eyes. Polands are non-sitters.

### The author writes:

"We have one Poland bantam who is completely scatty and almost impossible to catch. I wouldn't recommend this breed as very suitable for the garden."

### Margaret Burns now living in France writes:

"I kept a variety of chickens in a suburban garden in Beaconsfield, Buckinghamshire: my favourite was a Poland spangled bantam cockerel named Cheeky. He was very fierce with men including my husband. He lost us our window cleaner as he followed him to the top of his ladder pecking his heels. Once we were expecting visitors and had to pop out so we left a note saying, 'pour a drink and we will be back shortly'. When we returned our guests were all huddled in the kitchen. They had strolled into the garden with their gin and tonics and had thrown their drinks over Cheeky to protect themselves. Cheeky loved me and used to sunbathe with me on a lounger sitting on my lap and spreading his wings. He met a sad end aged ten as my daughter didn't lock the chicken house one night and he and three hens were killed. I believe Polands are known for their fierce tempers but I thought my cock adorable and very handsome."

## RHODE ISLAND RED

The Rhode Island Red originated in America on the farms of the Rhode Island Province and they were developed from Red Malays crossed with brown Leghorns. They were first exhibited in 1880 in South Massachusetts and in 1909 the British Rhode Island Red Club was established. The breed has been one of the most popular in this country for all purposes especially in the past when people kept hens for meat as well as for eggs. The male, being a gold, is particularly useful for crossing with hens and is used extensively nowadays for the development of the many hybrids on the market. Eggs are light brown or brown in colour.

Rhode Island Reds along with Sussexes and Leghorns were the breeds that people kept on a more commercial basis during and between the wars as this and the following account will testify:

*Gina Mackenzie from Leatherhead, Surrey writes:*

"With four daughters to educate in the 1920s and 30s my father needed extra income for school fees. So, having enjoyed keeping a few hens in a coop, my parents went for it in a bigger way and built four big barns to hold about 1,000 birds. The foundations were covered in broken glass and wire netting to deter rats – we also kept cats from good ratting stock. Each hen house was in two parts with windows on one side and nestboxes and perches on the other, with outside access for egg collecting. The second part of each house had a door which led into an outside area like a tennis court, so unless the weather was truly awful the birds could spend the day there and scratch or dustbathe as they liked.

Water was laid on and was used to fill dispensers which had iodine added, as the water came from Derbyshire which is deficient in it. Each barn had a big meal ark; cod liver oil was added to the mash in winter besides the grains and grit which were the routine feed. Father bought in day-old chicks, Rhode Island Reds, which came by train to one of the Nottingham stations. Until they were reasonably fledged they lived in special hayboxes with little netting runs so they were warm and safe. Any which were not laying were given to two of us to look after. We graded the eggs by hand using a wooden scale and sold them locally.

At about two years old the birds were ready for the pot though some had already been sold as roasters. Twice disaster struck with infected chickens so when the price of eggs dropped it was time to call it a day. Some forty years later, when our house was gone and the fields were 'executive housing', a resident asked one of my sisters who had stayed in the district why he kept digging up bits of coloured glass in his garden. She was certainly able to tell him.

Even now I still think that one of life's lovely sounds is of hens contentedly crooning."

*Roger Phillippo from Cambridge writes*:

"During and just after the war we had about 4,000 contented hens, all egg producers. They were a reddish-brown colour and were called Rhode Island Reds – this was in a time before road crossing had become such a hazard, saving me the confusion of having chickens named after a reserve in the middle of the carriageway and a long time before I was aware of the American place which had given its name to the breed. To spice up their lives a bit we introduced into their world an Indian Game Cockerel. He stood about three feet tall and was all leg. He was a normal sized bird in the body area, but placed each side of him were these two enormous – albeit slightly bandy – legs; bandy enough, in fact to earn him the nickname Bandy Gandi and he turned out to be very spiteful. As soon as he saw anything human he would confrontationally bunch up his wiry feathers in front of him, challenging you in chicken language, 'C'mon, C'mon'. Even the vet agreed that he was unusually aggressive, pronouncing a severe case of Irritable Fowl Syndrome."

*The author writes:*

"I understand that Rhode Island Reds have recently been modified in breeding programmes so that they have lost some of their deep red colour, are less broody and smaller."

## ROSECOMB BANTAM

Only available as a bantam, the Rosecomb originated in Asia. It is small but sprightly with distinctive large white ear lobes and a rose comb. The wings are carried low and the breed comes in black, blue and white varieties. These bantams are mainly used for showing.

*Eris from Sussex writes*:

"I have recently started keeping some Black Rosecomb bantams. I have found these bantams to be very easy going, pleasant little birds. A flock of these tiny iridescent green jewels, with their bright red combs and white earlobes walking across the lawn is a lovely sight. What's more they have proved to be very decent layers for what is essentially a breed designed purely for visual enjoyment. A true miniature of the poultry world."

## SCOTS DUMPY

There are stories of Dumpies being in Scotland from 333BC, having been brought in by Phoenician traders. Scottish Clans living in remote villages valued them for their ability to raise the alarm. They were reportedly used by Clans on manoeuvres against the Romans. Unfortunately the Scots Dumpy is now very rare with fewer than 500 Dumpies remaining. They have very short legs and so tend to waddle around, giving the appearance of swimming on dry land. One advantage is they are not easily able to scratch up the flower beds. They are very friendly, tame birds and excellent layers and sitters. The Dumpies are black, cuckoo, white, brown, gold or silver. This, I think, is a great choice of bird for the small garden - an egg layer and a guard dog rolled into one and a garden that remains intact.

*Kirk Hunter from Central Scotland writes*:

"Dumpies are a really nice friendly breed. They see me coming from 100 yards and all run to the gate clucking and cooing to wait on me. My new Scots Dumpy hens are coming into lay. This morning I knew I was going to get an egg as one of the hens was acting strange going in and out of the house so I watched her and eventually she laid and came out and announced it so me and the cockerel Dumpy went for a look. I kept quiet and watched him he was making lovely soft noises and making a nest then he clutched the egg carefully in his claws and sat there making soft noises to himself for a couple of minutes and went back outside and let off a cockle doodle doo. I never thought they were so affectionate and caring to their hens and eggs. This is nature at its best. I am going to try and get myself a top class breeding stock and introduce the breed to as many people as possible."

*Kirk Hunter also writes:*

"I used to have a lovely Dumpy girl called Maggie. She was always a bit on the small side. When she came into lay she would get really upset and run in and out of the hen house.

The old cock at the time was a cuckoo cock called Rascal and he would watch this poor hen going through her labours with interest looking through the pop hole at her and I think he was worried for the young lass.

Then one day I was putting a bit of mixed veg out for them when I noticed that the cock was nowhere to be found. Having looked a bit harder I found him sat by the nest box in the shed. I thought he was ill and went to pick him up when he jumped to his feet and gave me an earful.

Maggie was in the nest box doing her usual panting and squeaking - she was the only hen I knew that made so much noise laying a egg.

I thought no more of it till I saw them come out of the pop hole together. After that I checked each time I was out and yes, he was always sitting there with her. It got to the point that she would come and get him when she needed to lay a egg. Sometimes he would be into something else and not keen to follow her but she would get louder and he would go.

After a while as long as he was sitting in the pop hole opening she was happy although the hens trying to get in were not.

This went on until she finished her laying season but when it all started again I swear he looked skyward when she called him.

They got divorced a few months later and she ran off to Scotland with a white Dumpy cock. They have had 34 young so far and the new hubby just lets her get on with it. Rascal never did show any interest in sitting with his new wives. I don't think he ever forgot Maggie. But his stress levels went down - that's for sure."

*Liz Anderson from Epworth, Lincolnshire writes:*

"Mikey, my bantam black Scots Dumpy, has a great nature. When his Mrs was expecting the patter of tiny feet she was in the broody run in his enclosure. She didn't come out of the run and each morning Mikey would come out of his shed take his other ladies to the feed then walk across to his Mrs Arwen. She was a bit off her food as her time grew near so he would stand by her feed cup (he was on the outside of the run) and cluck to her, pecking at the mesh behind her feed cup. He would get louder and louder until she got up and had something to eat and drink then he would be happy. The day after the chicks hatched he would walk around and around the run trying to give the chicks bits of food and he would always settle outside the run at night and we would have to put him to bed. In the end we gave in and put him in a larger run with mum and chicks. He was so happy I swear if a chicken could smile he was going to be the first. He was so gentle to them and he would let them under his feathers and on his back. He never fought with his own children when they grew into handsome cocks and people remarked on how wonderful he is walking around with ducks and chicks following him and to think he was going to be put in the freezer if I had not made that one phone call and saved him. He is a super little chap and a gentleman to the last. To this day if we hear loud clucking from the yard we always say, 'hey who is doing a Mikey?'"

## SCOTS GREY

The Scots Grey is a light, soft-feathered breed which originated in Scotland over 200 years ago. The breed was popular on Scottish farms and crofts supplying meat and eggs for the families. Known as a cottager's fowl, the Scots Grey was admired for its hardiness and ability to thrive in colder climates. It lays a large egg for the size of bird and the chicks mature quickly which used to be an advantage in the short Scottish summers. They are of course excellent foragers and their long legs were an advantage as they free ranged through the heather and long grass in Scotland. Cocks and hens are cuckoo coloured which means the feathers are barred – steel grey ground colour is barred with metallic black. The cocks have large upright combs as do the hens which sometimes flop slightly over. Available as large fowl and bantam, the breed does not enjoy a huge following of breeders even in Scotland. The hens lay white eggs. This breed is rare and is listed by the Rare Breeds Survival Trust as critical.

*John Cleverley from Hastings, East Sussex writes*:

"I have kept various poultry over the last 50 years including Old English Game, Wyandotte, Rhode Island Red, Sussex and Marans but I have not found any of these as endearing as the Scots Grey. I keep a small number of the bantams and although I have only had them for about two years, I am finding them to be first class little layers of good sized eggs. Although they are by no means wild or jumpy, I would recommend having a top to the area in which they are kept because they are capable of flying like a game bird, but generally speaking, given the right conditions they will be tame and friendly and above all entertaining and ornamental plus the cockerels strut around as if they own the place. After some effort I managed to find a breeder who was willing to part with a cockerel unrelated to my own and have just settled a cross bred bantam on some eggs.

I have read that the Scots Grey is classed as a non-sitter but all of my layers in this strain have been broody and one in particular goes broody regularly. I have found Scots Greys to be rare compared with many other strains but have on a few occasions spotted them at shows where they have picked up a good share of prizes. Apart from showing they are definitely my top breed. I would thoroughly recommend this delightful breed and if you like cuckoo marking then this may be the breed for you."

# SILKIE

Silkies originated in Asia, some believe in India, others think in China or Japan. They are famous for their broodiness and are covered in fine, silky fluff rather than feathers. Silkies are crested with feathers on the legs and they have five toes. Colours range from blue, gold and black to white and partridge. Ear lobes should rightly be turquoise and comb and wattles mulberry. Silkies are classified as a light soft-feathered large fowl but a small bantam version has been created which is docile and therefore popular with children.

Silkies are well known for making fantastic surrogate mothers. Unlike other breeds they will take on other chicks, even ducklings and don't mind when you add them to their brood. In times gone by, before incubators existed, Silkies were used as natural incubators by breeders not only of chickens, but also of pheasant, partridge and duck.

*Gill Stockman from Adgestone Vineyard on the Isle of Wight writes*:

"Pom-Pom, one of our gold Silkies, insisted on hatching her eggs out in the nesting box. This happens quite frequently so when the first chick is born I usually move it, with the eggs, and mum to a sensible place. When I heard Pom-Pom's first chick cheeping loudly, with the cheeps building up into a great crescendo, I thought something might not be quite right. Mum was out eating and drinking in a very laid back fashion, wiping her beak leisurely and thoroughly enjoying the day. She had no intention of going back, despite the now hysterical screaming of the chick. I took her, the chick, and the other eggs which already showed signs of hatching into a quiet cage with a small run and went out for an hour, hoping that when I returned, peace would be restored with Pom-Pom sitting on her eggs and chick!

Not likely! She was flying madly around the cage, the eggs were cold, and the vocal chick was lying wet and dead next to the water bowl. A lovely yellow Silkie chick. I couldn't believe it. I picked it up and took it into the house. 'Look what Pom-Pom's done,'

I cried out to my husband, 'she's let that chick die.' He was on the phone and didn't even hear me. I don't know what came over me but a sudden instinct was to try the kiss of life. I breathed lots of hot breaths into the chick's face but nothing happened. I did it again and again. I'm mad, I thought. I then fancied I saw a slight movement of its little beak. Did I? I rushed upstairs with it and blew the hairdryer on it from a safe distance. Did I see the beak move again? I kept this up for about five minutes but even though there did seem to be a sign of life, I thought that a chick barely an hour old, and so wet and dead could never recover.

I boiled the kettle, filled up my teddy bear hot water bottle and put it with the chick in a wine box. Soon the little chick was cheeping faintly. By the end of the day the cheeping was very loud and that evening I was relieved to put it under Monica, another gold Silkie hen who already had four five-day-old chicks. Teddy, named after the hot water bottle is now doing well and his mum went back to her nesting box and started on some fresh eggs."

*Sara Hayward from Canterbury, Kent writes about the Silkies she had when living on a farm in the Zimbabwe bush:*

"My late mother arrived one morning for a visit with two Silkie bantams in her car – pets for Tara, my two year old daughter. They were named Jonathan and

Jennifer, after the couple she had purchased them from. Jonathan became an absolute terror when Tara went to play in the garden. One of his favourite games was to ambush her as she went down her slide into the sandpit. He would stand with his head on one side watching as she climbed the steps, then rush round to the bottom of the slide, where he would pounce on her, causing her to shriek and run as fast as possible into the house. Quite who was the instigator of this, we never found out. Initially we believed the rooster was to blame, but one day, believing she was unobserved we saw Tara standing on the top of the steps to the slide yelling for him to come and play with her!

Her swing caused even more fun and games. A simple home made affair, it was strung from a beam in the open-ended barn where the bantams had their mesh enclosure and wooden house. Unfortunately, no amount of oiling could fix the rasping metallic noise it made as it went to and fro. No matter where he was in the garden, Jonathan could hear it, and he would race to the swing and stand directly in front of it. Chest puffed out, leaping up and down, he would peck wildly at Tara's bare feet each time the swing came his way. She would hold her little legs as high as she could and tease him by calling, 'Rooster, come and catch me,' – all the while shrieking in excitement. Years later, watching it on home video, Tara claimed the shrieks were those of terror!

Jonathan was the progenitor of a large clan who were left to roam the garden during daylight hours. This was fenced off from the surrounding bush and a farm worker was always present, even when we were not. The doors to the house were left open, as was common in those days in that country, and it proved to be the saving grace of his brood.

By the time Jonathan's clan numbered two dozen he had become a very grand rooster indeed, full of his own importance and very conscious of his duties in protecting his flock. Once released, early in the mornings, he would lead them round the garden. The back area was fairly small and dusty and close to the barn. The front was a long grassy downhill stretch leading to a sandy track and a dam. There were plenty of flower beds and rocky outcrops here, with several small indigenous trees but no real shelter for a very visible army of fluffy white bantams.

One day a hawk spotted them on his flight over the farm. Barely a day went by after that without him passing overhead looking for the chance to seize a Silkie. But he had reckoned without Jonathan, who used to post himself as a lookout on the nearest rock. As soon as danger loomed, he would set up a warning cry. This not only prompted whoever was home to tear out into the garden with a shotgun but was the signal for his flock to run for their lives.

Jonathan soon discovered that it was simply too far for his family, especially the babies, to get from the front garden to the back to seek shelter in the barn. Using his initiative, one day he headed for the French windows leading off the front garden into the sitting room. Realising what a safe haven this was, it became a regular sanctuary. Visitors were slightly surprised at times to have a couple of dozen bantams racing at top speed into the house – though to give Jonathan his due, he never overstayed his welcome, and once the danger was past, he would usher his brood back outside. His behaviour was that of a sheepdog herding his flock – and he was always the last one inside.

Miraculously, over the next couple of years, the hawk only managed to grab a baby chick once – despite my presence a few yards away. I did not have a weapon on me but cursed him loudly and shook my fist and amazingly he dropped it into a bush on the other side of the fence. I raced around to retrieve it and found that even more amazingly, the little bantam had survived unscathed.

Strangely, the constant presence of my two large dogs in the garden never deterred the hawk from his flight path over the house.

In addition to the two big dogs, we had two small Dachshunds, and the male of the pair, who arrived when Jonathan was fully grown, initially had 'issues' with the rooster. The two of them would face each other, and embark on a staring match to see who would back off first. But Jonathan was wise enough not to go for the young Daxie, who in turn never tried to harm the rooster. It was more of a game they played with each other and we learnt to ignore it once we realised neither would be harmed.

When my daughter was four, we left the farm and the country, never to return. The bantams were given away in pairs and groups to friends and sadly I do not know what became of Jonathan and his family. Since the chaos that descended on Zimbabwe's farms several years ago, I have not allowed my thoughts to dwell on the probable fate of Jonathan's descendants, especially as our area suffered the most violent invasions. I would rather hold the memory of a little girl who had her somewhat lonely childhood enriched by a rooster called Jonathan."

*Pat Hillyer from Hayle, Cornwall writes:*

"Shantung, a Silkie, decided to sit. After all it was February and there had been a couple of warm days. 'Ah,' she thought, 'Spring'. She's only the size of a crow and there she was perched on a mountain of eggs. A pinpoint on top of Everest. Within days, Polyester, her daughter, was in competition. She made a nest facing her mother and beak to beak they sat on their mountain peaks. Some 20 days later, they were playing bat and ball with a puff of yellow fluff. It survived and was quickly joined by two more fluff balls. Three chicks. Two doesn't go into three; leastways not very happily. The ensuing violence attracted next door's cat who took up his position by the pop-hole as a cheer leader.

I hurriedly tacked and tied netting round the feuding pair who were pecking, scratching and screeching amongst a shower of eggs and three little chicks. The other hens immediately tried to perch on my netting-barricade and one fell in. Feathers flew and with a squawk she was back out again, in an over excited state, she wouldn't stop squawking. Cockerel Spats (the boss cock) looking superb in the full flush of claimed fatherhood, strutted up and down crowing. It was bedlam. I prepared a nursery coop with a borrowed rabbit-run and a tea-chest and put the remaining eggs into the new nest, followed by the three chicks and after much scrambling around on hands and knees and pouncing, added the screeching mothers – it was disastrous – Shantung and Polyester, screaming abuse, were in a blind rage. The improvised structure swayed under the onslaught as clouds of feathers, eggs and chicks shot in all directions. In a survival bid, the chicks squeezed through the inch mesh into the main run. Mother hens, falling over scattered eggs, fought to the death. Or would have done so, had not Shantung collapsed in an exhausted heap; whereupon Polyester paraded her ranting ear-splitting victory.

I rescued the chicks and when all was quiet, popped them back into the nest. Polyester sat on them and every time Shantung moved, she attacked her. Something had to be done. I sought advice. I visited a poultry breeder who advised me to separate them immediately and sold me a rather expensive chicken ark suggesting I put Shantung with one chick into the new ark and divide up the eggs. Ideas, even apparently good ones, don't necessarily work out in practice. The best I could do was to push Shantung out into the main enclosure for her own safety and my sanity, thus leaving Polyester with all three chicks. I removed the remaining eggs and feeling like a murderess, dropped them into the dustbin with a little prayer.

Shantung, in the throes of postnatal depression, sulked in the henhouse, refusing to come out. Meanwhile, Polyester preened and paraded with the chicks and savaged my hand when I put food in and replenished the water; the raptor genes very much in evidence. The picture, so often found in a child's reader, of a lady in long, floral skirts calmly scattering corn from a basket to clucking hens, is all fantasy.

Polyester was not a good mum. Within a fortnight, she abandoned her babies; rudely pushing past me one day when I went to put some lettuce leaves in. she never gave a backward glance."

*Liam Kelleher from Birmingham writes about his Silkie hen:*

"She went broody and had six eggs. Unfortunately only one of these chicks hatched. Two months passed and I had a few ducklings hatched in the incubator so I brought the chick up to the house to teach the ducklings how to eat and drink. After about a month I brought the chick and ducklings back down and the Silkie accepted them all, protecting them, showing them food etc. Now a few months on and I have just introduced two chicks (two weeks old) and six ducklings (one week old) to the Silkie. It seems like they've been there all along. She is a really good foster mother."

Silver
Appenzeller
hen

Lavender
Araucana
bantam

Barnevelder
hen

Young
Fayoumi
cockerel

Gold
Brahma
hen

Jersey Giant hen

Buff Pekin
bantam

Blue Orpington hen

Scots
Dumpy
hen

Speckledy
hybrid
hen

Young
Marans
bantam

Buff
Sussex
bantam

A group
of
Sumatras

Vorwerk
hen

Two Welsummer bantams

My son,
Hamish
with our
gold-laced
wyandotte
bantam

A pair of blue-laced wyandotte bantams

Bluebelle hybrid hen

Black
Rock
hybrid hen

## SULTAN

This is an ornamental breed originally from Turkey, where it was found strutting around the Sultan of Constantinople's palace gardens. Sultans in this country are all descended from a crate imported by a Miss Watts in 1854. Sultans are a rare breed and all are white with feathered five-toed feet, head crests and faces covered with thick muffling. Hens lay white eggs.

*Eris from Sussex writes:*

"Sultans are the figurehead of the Rare Poultry Society. In my experience they are very nicely behaved birds and a joy to own, the females in particular becoming very friendly. The only drawback I found was the huge feet feathering that on occasion would break. If they had blood on their feathers this would attract unwanted attention from the other birds."

## SUMATRA

This is rather an exotic breed which originated in Sumatra. It is a long-tailed game fowl, which has a graceful pheasant-like appearance. Sumatras are black with a lovely green sheen and have dark purple combs and faces. Young cockerels kept together are likely to start fighting. Hens are prolific layers of white eggs. Sumatras are available as bantams and although black is the more usual colour blue Sumatras have also been developed.

*Eris from Sussex writes:*

"A friend had a batch of Sumatras that she had kept in pens, without them producing a single fertile egg. When she moved them to new premises, now being permitted total freedom, they promptly produced many fertile eggs and raised a large batch of chicks without any artificial assistance."

**SUSSEX**

This is an old breed derived from the Old Sussex fowls which were bred in Victorian times for their meat and eggs. The oldest variety is in fact the Speckled Sussex. The Light Sussex was developed using Brahmas, Cochins and Dorkings. The Sussex is a heavy soft-feathered breed which lays tinted eggs. During the war Light Sussexes along with Rhode Island Reds seem to have been popular breeds to keep for the dual purpose of eggs and meat. Nowadays Buff and Silver Sussexes are popular colours and are available as bantams or as large fowl.

*Marion Smith from Sedbergh, Cumbria writes:*

"Two of our Light Sussex hens are great buddies and often go to lay together, sitting one on top of the other, chirruping and growling softly, sometimes each with its head under the other's wing. This performance does not always produce two eggs, however, but there are always two declarations, each claiming the credit. Sometimes one of these hens must find a little difficulty in finally parting with her egg as she will stand up with bent hocks and do a series of 'Evening All' type dips before finally delivering the egg from a standing position, wings hunched up as though her hands are in her pockets and an expression of fierce concentration on her face."

*[I thought this was a great description of a hen laying an egg.]*

"Our rooster, Gigli, is a great character, very friendly and inclined to stand on the garden table and tap on the sitting room window to tell us when it is feeding time. He would dearly like to be a house bird and is frequently found in the kitchen if the house door is left open. When my husband digs the garden all the hens arrive from the field and he has to shake them off his fork as he lifts it, such is their impatience to get to the worms he is uncovering. We find Light Sussexes very friendly, tame and placid, sheltering in the sheep shed in bad weather and sitting on the backs of the sheep for warmth."

*David Roden from Welwyn Garden City, Hertfordshire writes:*

"Speckle, a Light Sussex bantam was very tame and used to come in the back door for titbits. She lived to the great age of 19 years and was active until the last when she simply passed away and I found her underneath the perch one morning. Her friend, a Buff Sussex bantam was less tame but bought at the same time. At the age of 18 years she produced one egg after many years not laying. She then went broody and sat for a couple of days before wandering around the garden again. She obviously thought she had a brood and clucked to call her imaginary chicks. Sadly she died recently at the age of 20 but I am sure that to live to such a great age our two hens were happy."

*Nicholas Howard from Surrey sent me an amusing story about his Sussex bantam:*

"We keep five hens. On this particular day I cleared out the hen house and put the wood chips in a large sack. I then went round to the front of the house and got the car ready to go to the local dump. I put the sack into the car with the top folded over and merrily went on my way to the dump.

When I arrived I tipped the large sack out on to the recycle heap and to my amazement and total shock one of my hens jumped out into the heap. Once I realised what had happened, I jumped on to the heap to retrieve my hen and my legs went straight into all the muck up to my knees.

While this was going on an old man was getting out of the car next door to me. He looked amazed at me and the hen and all I could think of saying was 'that she loved me so much that she did not want to stay at home.' The gentleman did not say a word, just looked at me as if I was mad. I managed to get the hen home, but forgot all about the other recycle material in the car which I had brought home again."

*The Daily Mail reported the following story on 15 July 2005:*

"Rooster Coburn – the biggest cockerel in Britain – has shown his power by fighting off a fox which broke into his coop and threatened his hens. The Light

Sussex cockerel – 3ft tall and 25 lbs – beat the intruder to 'within an inch of his life', said owner Tim Stone, who was woken by the noise of the battle in Shepton Mallet, Somerset. He said, 'There was a yelp and I saw the fox limping off. The whole area was covered with blood and red fur and Rooster was strutting around like a winning boxer after a fight'."

## VORWERK

The Vorwerk was developed in Germany in 1900 by Oskar Vorwerk and is classed as a rare breed. Vorwerks make excellent hens for the garden because they are medium size, attractive and thrive very well on less rations than other breeds of the same size. Vorwerks are buff coloured with black belted marking which means the neck and tail feathers are black. They are alert, very active and excellent foragers. They lay white eggs and go broody fairly easily. Vorwerks are good flyers so do not usually like to be confined.

*The author writes:*

"I have a Vorwerk, named Val, hatched from a Domestic Fowl Trust egg – she is head of the pecking order and always first in the queue for titbits. She will also follow me around when I have a fork or spade in my hands so that she can be first to grab the worms or grubs from any overturned soil. She has sat patiently on eggs over the last few years, successfully rearing broods of chicks – the year before last she was obviously keen to fit in two lots of chicks – having reared her first lot, after five weeks (which was really a little early for her chicks to leave her) she decided she had had enough, started pecking them before beginning to lay another clutch of eggs. Last year, however, she hatched a little Poland bantam and a Pekin. The Poland in particular was very timid and Val stayed with her and the Pekin for four months! (The average span of time for a hen to stay with her offspring is 6 – 8 weeks)."

## WELSUMMER

Although Welsummers are traditionally associated with Welsum in Holland the breed was originally created in the area along the river Ysel, just north of Deventer. The breed was developed in the early 1900s, about the same time as the Barnevelders. In the early development of the breed Barnevelders were used. Welsummers arrived in England around 1928.

A light, soft-feathered breed, they lay large dark brown eggs with a matt shell rather than the glossy shell of the Marans. The colour of the eggs will vary slightly depending on the strain but these are probably the darkest brown of all egg layers.

Welsummers were originally all a red partridge colour - the cocks always have reddish brown mottling on their black breasts. However there is now a silver duckwing variety. Welsummers are very active foragers, so won't eat you out of house and home. They don't lay as many eggs a year as some other breeds, especially the hybrids and won't lay in the winter but they will go on laying for longer. Welsummers are meant to be non-sitters but a friend's Welsummers seem to go broody regularly - this implies that a lot depends on the strain.

*Clemmie Perowne, from Gillingham, Norfolk writes:*

"Welsummers are a charming breed not just because they are beautiful to look at (strikingly simple at first glance with their chestnut bodies and golden necks, but look closer and you see that each feather is quite ornately decorated) but also because of their wonderful flowerpot red eggs.

The birds are perky and interested in everything, incredibly inquisitive wanting to know exactly what you are doing. They can be drama queens... launching themselves across the garden in a flurry of flapping wings and cycling legs when something 'spooks' them but I think that adds to their character and appeal.

Finding my first brown egg from a Welsummer was like finding gold! And even now the novelty hasn't worn off. I think the eggs are so gorgeous to look at... like a piece of art... that sometimes I can hardly bring myself to crack them open. Each one is different - some with freckles, some with graduation of colour from top to bottom, each one a masterpiece.

As you can probably tell, I love my Welsummers! I have other breeds, but they are one of my definite favourites."

# WYANDOTTE

The first variety of the Wyandotte was the silver-laced and it originated in America named after a tribe of North American Indians. The Wyandotte tribe still have a few members living in Northern Oklahoma today. It is not absolutely clear which breeds were used to develop the Wyandotte but it was probably Cochins. The Wyandotte was introduced into Britain in the late 1800s and in the early 1900s was very popular along with the Leghorn as an egg laying breed.

There are a variety of colours available nowadays which include gold, buff and blue-laced, partridge, Columbian and silver-pencilled. Varieties have been developed by crossing different breeds with Wyandottes – for example the partridge Cochin and gold-spangled Hamburgh males were crossed with silver-laced females to produce the gold-laced varieties and the Columbians came about by crossing white Wyandottes with Brahmas. In recent times the Wyandotte bantams have become more popular than the large fowl. They are so pretty that I think they make an excellent choice for the garden.

Wyandottes are a heavy, soft-feathered breed and lay tinted eggs. They tend to have lots of fluffy down feathers round their behinds which add to their attractiveness. They go broody rather easily and can be very persistent about it. However they make excellent mothers. Wyandotte bantams are a good choice if you have children as they tend to be friendly and easily tamed. The cocks are not aggressive and in general the bantams are not flighty and easily confined if you have no alternative.

*The author writes:*

"We have kept silver and gold-laced wyandottes in the past and have lost a few to a fox – the drawback was that the fox seemed to pick out the speckly black and white appearance of the silver-laced wyandottes (maybe it was easier to distinguish these coloured bantams in the field at dawn) over and above all our black bantams which remained untouched. Our wyandottes have never been particularly tame but our two gold-laced wyandottes (hatched out of eggs bought from the Domestic Fowl Trust) are really tame and friendly and leap on to your lap or shoulder as soon as you sit down outside and if you have any food in your hand it soon disappears."

# HYBRIDS

There are many hybrids now on the market which have been bred to be specifically good at egg laying but after two years of intensive laying, production of eggs will decrease. Hybrids were originally developed for intensive production and kept in battery conditions – the brown egg layers were based on the Rhode Island Red and the white egg layers on the White Leghorn. These have various trade names such as Shaver and ISA. ISA Warrens however are brown-feathered hybrids that have been specifically bred for free range.

Recently other hybrids have also been developed for free range conditions and also to look attractive in the garden. One of the most successful is the Black Rock. They are a true first cross hybrid, bred from selected strains of Rhode Island Reds and Barred Plymouth Rocks. Peter Siddons of Muirfield Hatchery in Scotland acquired the breeding stock from breeders in America in 1973. The Hatchery have agents spread over the UK with Black Rocks for sale but of course there are no cockerels available because Peter Siddons remains the sole breeder. Black Rocks have a good covering of feathers which protect them in all weather conditions. They also have a highly developed immune system and seem to be less prone to red mite than other breeds. They love being outside in all weathers. They do not go broody as this trait has been bred out of them and although egg production which is fantastic in the first two years may decrease thereafter, Black Rocks are hybrids that do manage to go on producing eggs and may live for up to ten years. Black Rocks are either black or ginger (with a ginger breast and attractive ginger and black lacing).

Bovans Nera is another hybrid, reasonably similar to Black Rocks. There are many other hybrids being developed with different names such as Calder Rangers, White Stars (developed from Leghorns and layers of white eggs) and Rhode Stars (from a Rhode Island Red). Meadowsweet Poultry Services have agents across the country and their range includes Bovans Nera (Black Star), Meadowsweet Ranger, Starlight (Marans Cuivree), Bluebelle (Rhode Marans and a layer of dark brown eggs), Daisybelle and Speckled Star (French Cuckoo Maran, also a layer of dark brown eggs). All these hens lay between 220 and 320 eggs a year. Cyril Bason Poultry supply a number of Hybrid layers but are also the sole breeder of Speckledy, Hebden Black and Calder Ranger.

There are also various autosexing breeds that have been developed and their names all end in –bar. These have been bred so that chicks can be sexed as soon as they have hatched by their down colouring. The first of these was the Cambar and was a cross between the Gold Campine and the barred Plymouth Rock. The barring is sex-linked and there is a double dose in the male and a single dose in the female – this means the male chick is paler with a blurred pattern of markings compared to the female chick. Recognised breeds are the gold, silver and cream Legbar (the Cream Legbar is a crossing which involves the Araucana and therefore lay blue eggs); the Rhodebar (from Rhode Island Red); Welbar (from Welsummer) and Dorbar (from Dorking).

*A Black Rock Hen*

*Julie Watson from Halifax writes:*

"We have four hens – two Black Rocks: Catherine of Aragon and Elizabeth and two White Stars: Mary and Ann Boleyn (our daughter is doing the Tudors in history). Each of the girls have their own personality and are incredibly friendly. We did know that the Black Rocks would be but the White Stars have become friendly too. Elizabeth always comes and inspects when you clean out the hen house, making sure you do a good job. Annie goes in the food store given half a chance. Mary is an escape artist. Fed up with tidying up after them my husband fenced off their part of the garden. Mary kept finding ways of escaping even performing a limbo under the fence. The others watched her but never followed. We have nicknamed her Steve McQueen.

Last summer we often found them sitting on the coir door mat in the porch soaking up the sun and they would give you such a look if you wanted to get past them. Our poor cats took to coming and going through a window.

Whilst watching them recently from an upstairs window I saw them chase away some crows. Initially the crows would not go, so a White Star went to the coop to collect her sister and with the arrival of all four hens the crows flew away."

*Susan Peill from Pickering in North Yorkshire writes of her Black Rock hen:*

"Agnus MacPherson (affectionately named after my husband's Scottish nanny, for her caring and busy personality) lived with us for three years, producing delicious brown eggs. When her eggs were no longer forthcoming she retired to the garden, her job now included maintaining the herbaceous borders, keeping the plants pest free and well manured. A frequent visitor to the kitchen door, Agnus would receive scraps of food, in return she would chatter away as if to gossip about the events taking place in the garden, I imagined her with arms crossed over her large fluffed out chest!

Agnus became very much part of the family, often spotted in the corner of photographs, observed under the garden table at barbecues, picnics and parties, even mentioned in Christmas cards. However, I had to draw the line, when one summer's afternoon, I was resting in bed following a nightshift working as a nurse at the local hospital. I had reached the twilight zone when one is neither asleep nor awake, suddenly I had the feeling I was not alone! A feeling of being watched swept over me! There she was – Agnus sitting on the end of the bed, ready with chest fluffed out and a story to tell! I do need to point out, although it was summer and windows were open, to get to the bedroom Agnus would need to negotiate the top half of a stable door, a baby gate and a flight of stairs, no problem to her obviously, but I would have taken her word for it, a calling card on the bedroom carpet was a little unnecessary!

Sadly the same summer Agnus was to meet her demise. One morning she came rushing to the kitchen door to inform me of the arrival of our large and handsome black cockerel. She made a real commotion, telling me with horror and much squawking of the cockerel's antics, out there she gestured with chest and wings fluffed out. He was in the orchard demonstrating his intentions to the other hens. Unfortunately the cockerel's persistent showing off advertised to the local fox the availability of a tasty chicken supper and Agnus disappeared before dusk."

*Rachel Elvidge from Maldon, Essex writes:*

"Well, I'm very new to all this, but with three small children and a dog, I need a breed that is bombproof. While some others have died of shock from coming to live here (sad but true) my Black Rocks seem to thrive on all the frenetic comings and goings.

Yesterday my five year old decided to take one of them down the slide on her lap.

Black Rocks are noisy blighters, but I love their characters. They are both really inquisitive, and brave, always the first out to forage, or to find an escape

114

route into next door's garden. They're superb layers, an egg a day, and they are waterproof, which makes them less depressing to look at when it rains. In fact, I think they are quite attractive in a sort of evil Bond-villain kind of way.

I can't say they are very affectionate; they are always trying to eat my toes (and my toddler), but they always come and see what I'm up to and they are certainly company.

To me, they are the ideal pet. You can ignore them and they get on fine. If you want to interact with them they are always up for being carried about or helping out with the weeding. Their eggs are the icing on the cake. In fact, I find myself looking at the dog and thinking, 'And what exactly do you contribute around here?'"

*Anne Perdeaux from Upavon, Wiltshire writes:*

"One of my Black Rock hens had a particularly nasty encounter with a dog, just a couple of weeks after we got our first chickens. Once again my husband wasn't around and on Sunday morning we experienced an invasion by two Jack Russell terriers. Fortunately, I arrived in time to eject them and they didn't actually harm the chickens, apart from poor Marilyn losing some tail feathers. I then spent a couple of hours searching for 12 chickens who had vanished in all directions. I was concerned that in their panic they might have got out and grabbing a tin of corn, ran up and down the road calling 'chook, chook chook,' which had no effect, apart from on my reputation. Eventually some began to reappear but the three Black Rock hens remained missing. I'd just about given up, having lost most of the day and missed lunch too, when they came out of hiding (behind a wheelbarrow) and began to prepare for bed. With great relief I watched them eat their final corn for the day, knowing that as dusk fell (which this being November, would be early) they could all be shut in safely and I could indulge in a long awaited cup of tea.

Suddenly another dog appeared and this one meant business. Once again chickens scattered everywhere but he managed to grab one of the hens who had hidden so cleverly. I can still hear her screams. She struggled to get away and escaped into the hen house where the dog followed her to finish the job. Angry and upset I grabbed the dog and, having pointed out the error of its ways, returned it to its owners. The hen was still alive, huddled in the nest box but her skin was badly torn. I removed her to a cardboard box and looked for the others. As it was now nearly dark I had visions of spending the night looking for them, but fortunately they all gradually and nervously came back to roost. Once they were in, I was able to examine the injured hen more closely. It was quickly evident that her wounds were beyond any first aid I could offer and that the sensible option would be a speedy despatch. Easier said than done. I've since been told that it's very easy to kill a chicken – like it's very simple to programme the video – if only you know how. It seemed such a shame too, especially after she'd hidden so well after the first attack, but then something had to be done. I wondered whether I could 'phone a friend' on a winter Sunday night and ask for help in chicken euthanasia and if so, which friend? Finally I phoned – the vet! On a Sunday… He kindly agreed to see the patient so I loaded her into the car and off we went. The vet explained that I'd already incurred the worse part of what would be a large bill from his out of hours examination. The cost would be similar whether he tried to stitch the wounds or put her to sleep, although she may die of shock anyway. She had a shot of antibiotic, another of painkiller, the vet stitched, I paid and the chicken made a full recovery. She went on to lay the biggest and brownest eggs of the lot and is still the hen most likely to be at the forefront of any eggscapades. I call her 'Naomi' – a very expensive black bird."

*Adrian Porter from Buckinghamshire writes:*

"The chickens were happily clucking this morning but it was not always the case. I was a newbie just a few months ago who has learnt quickly. I always wanted to keep chickens ever since my mother regaled me with stories about her own experiences in the war. Everyone kept chickens then, it was the only way to have fresh eggs and food was scarce at the best of times. Her chickens were kept in our large London garden and she warned me that it was hard work, going out every morning collecting the eggs and my Gran used to make some hot mash in the winter months. My father-in-law took me to task as well and sat me down to give me an hour's lecture on all the things that I would have to do including all the diseases that I needed to keep an eye on. It seemed that I would need the expertise of a vet and the constitution of a miner to be able to enjoy the simple pleasures of keeping some clucking hens.

For a while I did nothing. I had been beaten into submission. However, there was always a nagging voice in my head and we decided to take the plunge. My wife persuaded me to order a hen coop and we took some advice from my father-in-law's gardener on which sort to get. He promised to get us some hens and to generally sort out our needs. The coop we finally chose was the biggest and most luxurious coop in the brochure. If Michel Winner was a chicken he would be writing rave reviews about this coop, or so it seemed. It was an enclosed coop with a cosy nesting box upstairs for at least six birds, a small ladder led down to the scratching area below. We didn't want our hens to suffer some small ark-like coop - the fact that this coop was going to cost an arm and a leg would have shocked my mother who was used to making do from the war and had never changed. I was so excited to order it that I forgot to ask how it was going to be delivered and whether I would have to assemble it, a frightening thought as I am hopeless at DIY.

In spite of the promise of six weeks' waiting time, a man turned up only a week later, took the flat packed coop off the lorry and to my relief put it all together with only a cup of coffee for extra payment.

Even though it was a luxurious hen house it seemed quiet cramped in the scratching area. The hens would obviously want a bigger garden. So to give them more room we put some fencing around the coop so we would be able to let them out into a larger area during the day; this gave them more scratching and a feeding area.

A few days later, David the gardener brought us four lovely hens - two light Sussex and two Rhode Island Red. He had bought them from the poultry market that he goes to and they were 'point of lay'. He gave us some feed and some dishes to put the feed and water in. There was also some 'road chippings' that he assured us were an essential part of the hens' diet. They weren't really road chippings of course.

All settled in nicely and the hens all got on together like a hen house on fire, we fed them and watered them and they did some gentle clucking. There was a slight difficulty in getting them to go to bed every night. We had a devil of a job catching them and shoving them in their bedroom, they squawked and ran round the small enclosure and didn't want to get caught at all. But after one night they got the idea and the next night we just looked at them and they dutifully lined up like school children in a playground and walked up the ladder to bed.

We still wanted another two and after looking at various books and the internet we felt that Araucana fitted the bill with their coloured eggs. David couldn't find any so we relented and asked him to use his judgment to buy another two hens that would be interesting and complement the others.

Then one day I came home from work and heard some squawking from the coop, I couldn't believe the change. There were two large black chickens in the bottom area of the coop and the others had been forced to go upstairs. They were loud, clucking madly, bullies of the sixth form that had marched into the school and were keeping all the other pupils under their thumb. In the back of the coop were two large eggs obviously delivered by the new girls. When they wanted to go into the nesting box to lay, they chucked and pecked out the others. Talk about ruling the roost. We named them Hitler and Himmler. I phoned up David that night. He told me that they were called Black Rock. They were huge in comparison to our other sweet hens and, with their big red combs, were strutting around proudly.

'Are you sure they are hens?' I asked, '...they look so big.'

David sounded rather withering on the phone, 'you did say they had laid some eggs,' he said.

Yes, well I told you I was a bit of a newbie when it came to chicken keeping!"

***Carole Miller from Farnham, Surrey writes about how she obtained her new hybrids:***

"Maybe we could put some chickens on our wedding list? What better gift for friends and family to bless us with than fresh eggs every morning? How difficult could it be to keep a couple of feathery friends who can pretty much look after themselves and the cats seem to hang in there, so surely two chickens can't be that difficult?

After much trawling of the internet we found a company that would supply the whole kit and caboodle including hens, a Ginger Nut Ranger and a Miss Pepperpot (from a Rhode Island Red and a Barred Plymouth Rock) with a compact and bijou plastic hen house (called an Eglu) to boot. The Company, Omlet Ltd also agreed to the hassle of managing phone calls from our wedding guests making contributions.

So out went the invites, with details of our desire to become the next Tom and Barbara Good, and the chicken package was quickly snapped up. In fact our friends were so generous, or at least bemused, by the idea that we could have had at least three hen houses.

Those relegated to buying towels and bed linen made their protests known and bought books on chicken keeping instead, or maybe they were just fearful for the well-being of the poor animals due to our prior experience of keeping chickens being non-existent.

So, formalities, vicars and 'I dos' over and the second big day arrives when we take delivery of the new members of our household. Some friends arrive with their three and five year old daughters to witness the occasion and we wait and we wait. Just as it turns dark the chicken delivery van appears and the delivery guys stumble about in our garden trying to put up the plastic space age house and run. Several clips and pins and curvy bits of wire later and we have a pod-like hen house at the end of our garden - now for the chickens.

By now it truly is dark so we all huddle around the security light as the chickens are taken out of their boxes. The kids have been told they can name one each and Jess, being the oldest immediately bags her 'I'm the eldest' rites and names the first one out of the box 'Hannah' who's full of life and a pale shade of ginger. Gemma then plays her trump card and the next chicken, who's as black as the night, gets christened 'Rosie' - so let's get this right, the Rosie coloured one is called 'Hannah' by default the other one must be 'Rosie' – Oh God, this is what you get when you let two under fives make lasting decisions for you!! We then get a quick run down on chicken welfare, although by this time it really is dark and the temperature's dropping and the man doing the explaining has to keep waving a chicken at the security light so that we can see the vital components of each chicken as he provides an overview of the physiology of the domestic hen.

There's lots of talk of scratching and claws and holding their knees (chickens have knees?) apparently to minimise the risk of injury(!) and then we get asked if we'd like to hold 'Rosie'. Images of a missed opportunity to put a pair of those huge falconry gloves on our wedding list flash through our minds and we mutter something about maybe holding them tomorrow when they've settled in (and we've had chance to procure some of those nice thick falconry gloves!). However, Jess being devoid of fear at the grand age of five is soon cradling 'Rosie' in her arms and loving every minute of it, so fearful of humiliation we step up to the mark, prove we're not scared (honest!) and take the chicken by the (metaphorical) wings and knees and anything else we can do to hold them together. The chickens seem to be braced and ready for incompetent humans holding them and behave extremely well....we both walk away unscathed.

Just before we get left to be full-time carers to our new family members we're asked if we'd like their wings clipped. Seeing as neither of us fancy having to coax them down from trees or relish the prospect of having to ask the neighbours 'Can we have our chickens back please?' we agree that this is probably the best course of action. Our chicken delivery man quickly administers a feather trim, courtesy of our kitchen scissors, that Vidal Sassoon would be proud of. There's a bit of clucking, a few flying feathers and children looking on in consternation but no one seems to come out of the process mentally scarred, although we may have to employ a mobile hairdresser to assist when their feathers grow back.

After the fuss, journey and feather trimming Hannah and Rosie decide enough is enough and take themselves off to bed for the night, we take ourselves inside to thaw out and open a bottle of wine to come to terms with the additional responsibility we've just taken on.

Several weeks pass and we're getting quite good at being Mum and Dad to the feather children. Rosie and Hannah follow us around the garden as we dig in the depths of winter trying to get the garden of our now slightly less dilapidated house, into some sort of order. Reiss and Jasper, the cats, get too close to Rosie and are rewarded with a squawk and peck on the nose, which teaches them a lesson they won't forget in a hurry. Then we have a break-through…we get an egg and the next day another. Big yolks as yellow as the sun and perfectly formed shells, every day our 'girls' produce us two beautiful organic eggs. To start with we have eggs with everything, weekends are a cholesterol and protein roller-coaster, it seems such sacrilege to waste any after all that clucking, scratching and preening to make them. As time goes on the eggs get bigger, I swear I see Hannah's eyes watering, how an animal of that size can produce something that size day after day is beyond me.

Several months later and friends turn up for weekends toting duvet, pillows, a change of clothes and egg-boxes. The neighbours think we're quite mad but queue up to look after the menagerie whenever we're away in return for fresh eggs for breakfast. Most of all, though, we're just happy living our married, organic, protein fuelled lives with our girls who really were the gift that keeps on (and on and on) giving – bless them!!"

*Beryl Russell from Windsor, Berkshire writes*:

"Gnasty Gnorc is a Bovans Nera - she is a real character, and rules the garden. At present she is chasing and pecking me, because I figured her babies were well feathered enough to go it alone and put her back with the layers. Bad move. They are fine, but she hasn't forgiven me. She bears grudges for a long time.

I was told Bovan Neras don't go broody. Well, not in their first three years they didn't. Blax went broody last year, and mournfully clucked away at her dummy eggs for seven weeks, while I tried desperately to get some real eggs for her without success.

This year two went broody. First Gnasty Gnorc, who is a terror. She hatched three Marans X Araucana and four Cream Legbar X Black Rock.

Then Blax sat on one batch of eggs which were no good. Realising this at day 10, I rushed to get another dozen eggs. Six were infertile, two died at about 14 days, two at hatch, and the last two had to be helped out. Only one very pretty Welsummer survived. Blax is an exceptionally good mother too.

I have found them to be excellent free rangers, out in all weathers, and apart from one nasty bout of red mite, they have been exceptionally healthy. They are feathered egg machines. Average 300+ eggs per bird, per annum. They lay good sized eggs with a tendency to double yolkers in the spring. I think they are good hens for someone who wants a lot of eggs."

***John Hancox from York writes about his experiences with hybrids versus Maranses:***

"My experience started when I rented an allotment. I made a hen hut and created a large run. My initial flock consisted of four young Marans hens. The eggs were fantastic, a lovely chocolate brown colour with rich orangey yellow yolks and a marvellous flavour … shortly after the Maranses had taken up residence I was given two young hybrid hens which needed homing – the type of hen used in deep litter houses. The difference between the Maranses and the hybrids was amazing – the Maranses would eat huge quantities of food and produce an egg when it suited them. With the approach of winter egg production virtually ceased until spring. The hybrids on the other hand laid one egg a day more or less without fail even through winter and seemed to eat half the food. The Maranses lived to be quite old birds whilst the hybrids were past their best after two years. No doubt they were burnt out with egg production, the egg shells becoming thin and corrugated.

After a while, following the odd hen bereavement, I needed some new hens and purchased six hybrid day old chicks from the Hatchery in the village. I borrowed a broody bantam to educate them in normal hen activities and then let them loose in the garden at home. They were very entertaining but knocked hell out of the garden. On the allotment the favourite hen occupation when released from the run was to head for the tidy manure heap and in the space of a few minutes it was scattered far and wide. Their legs kicked manure backwards as if they were digging for victory. If you picked a hen up its crop would be bulging with a mass of worms and other goodies.

My father-in-law phoned me one day to say that a neighbouring farmer had a young cockerel looking for a home and in a weak moment I agreed to have him. On the appointed day, my six year old son and I collected him using a borrowed wicker cage. We went down to the allotment and I put the cage just inside the gate to the run and let the cockerel out, shut the gate, bent down to do up the straps on the cage to hear the announcement from my son, 'he's done them all, Dad!' This cock was a fine bird very haughty looking, being a rich golden colour and must have had some Indian game bird genes as he had long legs and stood very upright, a bit like the Road Runner in that cartoon.

One day when I was not concentrating he slipped out of the gate and in a second he was gone. The speed he could achieve was amazing and I thought that was the last I had seen of him but after a while I saw a red wattle-covered head about 60 yards away. He was keeping an eye on me. Any attempt to move in his direction and he would disappear.

After an hour of this hide and seek I had a moment of inspiration. The easiest way to control a bull is to let him have a cow to occupy his mind so I let the chickens out and within moments he had run back at full speed doing a couple of hens in the process. I then put them all back in the run with no further problems.

I always clip one wing on each of my hens to stop them flying. If you clip one wing they spill air on one side and turn in a circle dropping back to the ground. If you clip both wings lift is reduced but they can still fly and maintain direction.

Next I was given three bantams, one of which was my all time favourite. She was a shiny black hen but very small, being only about six inches high. What amazed me was that following the death of the cock she ruled the roost. She was certainly aggressive although her egg production was hopeless but sometimes you need a supervisor to keep an eye on things."

# CROSS BREEDS AND
# EX-BATTERY HENS

*Catharine Jessop from Bedfordshire writes*:

"I have three cross-bred hens which are completely free range in my Bedfordshire village garden of about ¼ acre. I am amazed at their resourcefulness in finding ways to escape from the garden (luckily my neighbours are tolerant and the hens always find their way back at night). However, I am a little concerned that they are developing an identity crisis from their happy co-existence with my three cats. They have taken to coming into the house through the cat-flap and I have caught them tucking into the Whiskas. More alarming still, I rescued a shrew from one of the cats and let it go in the garden, only to see it set upon by one of the hens which pecked it to death and set about eating it.

This being my first tiny flock (bought two years ago and haven't stopped laying yet) I certainly very much agree that hens are ideal as family pets – they need very little work, are cheap to feed, fascinating to watch and good company in the garden. The children love them and particularly collecting the eggs. The eggs taste far better as well as being fresher than supermarket eggs.

Going away on holiday has not been a problem since neighbours or local teenagers are usually happy to come in and shut the hens up at night and let them out in the morning, in return for the eggs."

*Janet Isherwood from Derbyshire writes*:

"It appeared that Houdini Hen, a feisty bantam cross had escaped again. Usually she would be back, safe and snug in the hen house by dusk, but this time, after nearly three weeks' absence, we feared the worst. Imagine our surprise when we heard the contented clucking and cheeping of a mother hen and her newly hatched chicks. Slight problem! The new brood was sited in the bottom of a hawthorn hedge surrounded by nettles and brambles. We formulated a plan of action; my husband would grab Houdini and armed with a washing up bowl, I would collect up the chicks. After all, it was paramount the new family should be inside the fox proof run.

As soon as my husband's outstretched hands came within six inches of the mother hen, she gave an ear-piercing squawk and shot off, whilst what seemed like dozens of fluffy chicks sprinted in all directions, cheeping anxiously.

There ensued a four hour hunt, involving endless silent waiting and lightening quick reactions, before we finally managed to settle mother and 16 chicks in the safety of the hen run. She'd hatched, and subsequently reared the chicks – four cockerels and

12 hens – all on her own in a hedge bottom. We were thrilled, albeit stung, scratched and bleeding from the escapade. We kept the most handsome cockerel and gave the other three away to distant good homes (their crowing was not conducive to good neighbour relations). The 12 sisters have been providing a surfeit of eggs every season and Houdini Hen still holds her own with all her offspring."

*[They were very lucky to have only had four cocks out of 16. On average at least half of these would have been cockerels.]*

### Dr Norman Sutcliffe from Leigh-on-Sea , Essex writes:

"Many years ago in the 1960s when I was a young doctor in General Practice, I was doing my home visits (as one did in those days!) and one was to see a farmer at a poultry farm. Having attended to my patient I came out of the house and heard a lot of noise coming from a huge poultry shed. Looking through the door I saw the hens being taken from the battery cages to go to the killing station.

 They were being very roughly handled and although their transfer was necessary if hens are to be kept in this way, I was appalled at the way it was done. I heard a leg break as a bird was pulled from the cage and I grabbed it and said, 'I'll have that one.' I was told it cost three shillings which I paid. I took her home and set her leg with two splints using the old wooden tongue depressors and sticking plasters – she looked a wreck – hardly any feathers and covered in peck wounds as she was obviously lowest in the pecking order in a cage containing four birds.

My children came back from school and asked, 'could they keep her?' and having been to Sunday school the previous Sunday and heard the story of Lazarus being raised from the dead, called her Lazarus – or affectionately Lazzy.

She grew into a lovely bird and was possibly a Black Leghorn. The leg healed perfectly but of course she had to learn to walk again – not having used her legs for so long.

She lived in her own little house and run in the garden – separately from our other hens, but she had free range of the garden during the day – and the kitchen where she seemed to spend most of her time. She laid eggs for a few years – frequently on the cushion on the kitchen chair.

The children adored her – spoilt her shamelessly – feeding her treats of chocolate and cream crackers as presents at Easter and Christmas. This was probably the cause of her demise as she got overweight, but lived with us for nine years. She must have been about 11 when she died.

Eventually she went off her legs and couldn't walk at all so the time had come to say goodbye. My wife said 'Don't wring her neck, I couldn't stand it' so I prepared the children and then gave her an injection of morphine (enough to kill most of the people in the road) and she went to sleep for three days, during which time one of my sons insisted she was hospitalised in his bedroom. After three days she woke up again. In the end the vet came in and did the job properly with his injection!

She is remembered with great affection in our family and taught the children a lot about animal welfare."

*David from Pudsey, West Yorkshire writes:*

"We had seven hens and one weekend they went AWOL – we phoned the local police who took the details down. Gone for ever – not a bit of it! Next day the police said they had a report that on a local council estate an irate father had found seven hens (white with bits of black) in his hut – his son later admitted the theft. The police took us in their white transit to the house and we identified six as we were not certain about the seventh. The police loaded up the van (a crew bus with seats) – each hen sat on its own seat and was driven the odd mile back home. The kids were delighted but the police weren't – as the sergeant pointed out, 'they've crapped on every seat!' Nervous passengers, I guess. We duly wiped away the offending guano and thanked the police for an excellent job. I would love to have seen the officer's report – a rather unusual case especially in an urban area such as Pudsey."

*[This was in 1981 – I doubt whether the police would have had time for such cases nowadays.]*

*Clare Gilchrist from Leicestershire writes:*

"I have a pair of lavender-coloured bantams that are part Marans, part Scots Dumpy and part Pekin. They are feather-legged and tiny but very hardy. The hen lays big eggs for her size that are pink-coloured. They are extremely friendly, following us around the garden, clucking and are very inquisitive – they've been in the house and conservatory more than once! The hen catches mice occasionally and the cock looks after her very well – calling her if he finds something tasty. They always make sure that they are back in the run and have put themselves to bed before it's dark and they adore worms. They are utterly adorable and everyone loves them."

*Judith Fusaro from Cupar, Fife in Scotland has black hens and white hens with one or two speckled brown ones and writes:*

"I keep chickens, or perhaps I should say that my chickens keep me – sane! My three teenage children and most of my friends think I am totally nuts, but they really are the funniest creatures, the chickens, not my friends!! Whenever they hear my voice they come flapping from all corners of the garden and at the moment we are collecting anything between six and eight eggs every day. They are totally free range, with around two acres to run around.

My most unusual story is of one little lady who insists on laying her egg every day in our scullery. She will sit outside on the window sill until someone opens the back door for her, comes inside and flies up onto the worktop where she will settle herself down for half an hour, lays and then squawks to get back outside again. Not even our two Labradors can scare her off!"

*Diana Rylatt from Worcestershire writes:*

"My Mum kept free range poultry over the years in a village garden. She had a selection of rescue chickens of assorted breeds, size and colour together with a one legged duck. She generally referred to them by description rather than name and this particular chicken was 'the little black hen'. She was the smallest of her haphazard brood and the only one that was even vaguely black. Her chickens were not altogether reliable as they would sometimes put themselves away at night with the chickens who were kept next door but one, and a local fox was a regular visitor. On this occasion the little black hen had gone missing at a time when she had been laying on a regular basis. She wasn't with the neighbours and the fox had not visited. She was found four days later underneath an overturned container together with an egg for every day she had been missing. How she got underneath the container remains a mystery but except for a particular thirst she seemed unharmed by her ordeal and continued her free range life for a number of years."

*Rowena Godwin writes:*

"This is an absolutely true incident -   Last year my husband and I stayed with some friends in their house in Umbria, Italy.  One day I decided to weed one of the raised flowerbeds and was soon joined by their six (to my eye) identical brown chickens, who together with 12 ducks and two turkeys were allowed to roam freely on the property. As I bent over the earth one of the chickens brushed against the right side of my face, in what I thought was a flurry of excitement at getting an easy lunch.

Several minutes later I felt a decided peck on my left ear. When I put my hand up to feel for any damage I discovered my pearl earring was missing. I then automatically put my hand to my other ear only to discover that the earring on that side too was missing. The most unlikely fact of all was that each of the gold butterflies still remained, stuck behind my earlobes (the proof is now in my jewellery box). Though I took a photograph of the chickens, and advised my friends to look out for anything shining in the grass, the guilty hens and their loot were never found."

***Nicki Bridge from Devon writes about her ex-battery hens*** [*I think she has done a wonderful job with them*]:

"When my six battery hens arrived late one evening they looked a sad sorry sight. I'd been warned what to expect but the reality hit me harder and I had a little cry. They were so tatty, hardly any feathers on some of them and they had grey combs and forlorn little faces. I was worried that perhaps I'd taken on too much. I immediately named one Turkey as she had a bare neck.

At first they were so frightened. I wanted to help them sleep in the right places and show them some affection but even going near them on the first day stressed them so much that I felt it kinder just to make sure they had soft straw to sleep on the floor, food and water and left them to it. Of course I couldn't help observing quietly round the corner. The next morning there were eggs everywhere! Very thin shelled, pale eggs. Not what I'm used to with my hens.

Over the next few days I saw big changes. They started to get some colour in their faces, they didn't run into the corner when I brought food, but ran to me eager for their treats. They were starting to trust me and it felt great.

The mash only diet only lasted for a day or two and they all quickly tucked into pellets, mixed corn and veggie treats. They also started to enjoy exploring outside when the sun wasn't too strong for their bare skin. It warmed my heart to see them chasing butterflies.

It's been just over a month now. They have successfully mixed with my other hens. I was a little worried about doing this but it went smoothly. The ex-battery hens are the strongest of my flock and definitely boss around the old girls. Feathers are starting to grow on bald patches and everyone is very happy and living a contented life. Since mixing them with the others, the ex-battery girls have started more normal chicken behaviour. They lay nice thick shelled, rich yellow yolked eggs in the nest box, sleep on the perches and scratch around in the dirt. I'm convinced they learn from each other.

This experience has been a positive one both for my family and the ex-battery girls. I wouldn't hesitate to have some more in the future. Apart from the initial tender loving care in the first couple of days, my girls haven't really required much more than normal hens from me. They've done all the hard work on their own."

### Tina Camfield from London writes:

"I have three ex-battery hens; I've had them since March. When I first got mine, they would only eat layers mash. They didn't recognise pellets as food! They were a bit fragile on their legs too, as they hadn't really had to use them in the cages. They didn't perch at all, but slept in the nest box, two of them still won't perch!

They had few or no feathers. One of them had a bare breast, and one a bare bottom and no feathers round her neck. I wanted to knit her a scarf! Their feathers are beginning to grow back now. After a week, we let them out into the garden an hour before sunset (supervised). They were very hesitant at first, but they soon got the hang of it, and the feel of grass under their feet.

Now, they live quite happily with my other five ladies, they all sleep in the same coop, and they eat layers pellets, and free range round the garden. They will jump up on our lap when we're sitting in the garden which gave my friend a bit of a fright! They also try to drink my tea! They are the friendliest of all my hens. I couldn't imagine life without my girls – all of whom are much loved pets."

**_Rosamund Young writes (from The Secret Life of Cows, published by Farming Books):_**

"In the winter the Land Rover is loaded up with hay and the hens try their hardest to cadge a lift. They know they are not supposed to so they peck round the wheels nonchalantly and wait for an opportunity when our backs are turned. One will usually manage to jump in and hide amongst the hay, and once, when the engine was running and we did not hear the triumphant singing, a hen got away with it and was not discovered until the hay was being unloaded ten miles away up in the fields. She tumbled out with a bale of hay and the wind buffeted her this way and that. The cows formed a circle of surprise round her but she was not at all intimidated. I picked her up and lifted her into the front of the vehicle, where she stood on the seat and looked round like a queen on an official drive-about. I resumed the hay distribution and found an egg."

*Also from The Secret Life of Cows, Rosamund Young writes*:

"When the Old Grey Hen was fifteen the fox ate two of her friends and damaged her leg severely. She was given medical attention and her leg was bandaged. For three days she ate nothing, however tempting, just taking frequent, small sips of water. On the fourth morning she ate a piece of bread and from then on never looked back, consuming every imaginable delicacy we could think of: raspberries and cream, butter, cheese, wheat, barley, milk, bread and dripping (her favourite), cooked beef, raisins etc. During the first four days and as it turned out, for more than a year after, our other two hens exhibited such genuine, loving and altruistic behaviour that we found ourselves marvelling.

They became her devoted bodyguards and when food was offered, they would stand by and watch until she had eaten all she wanted and only then would they eat themselves. They would walk about, pecking and investigating things but every few minutes one or both of them would hurry back to the grey hen's side to see if she was all right. They comforted her by gently moving their beaks up and down hers. She did not mind them enjoying themselves but became anxious if they went completely out of sight. The two friends, sisters of the same age and 12 years younger than the 'invalid' had not been particularly friendly to the old hen before her trauma: she was truly the eminence grise and perhaps they had been kept in line by her to a certain extent. But as soon as she was no longer able to fend for herself they changed utterly.

During all this time she did not move. She sat in a nest of hay in the garden all day and in a different nest in their pen at night. She learned how to ask to be carried to different locations in the garden by craning her neck in the direction her friends had gone, and by looking at us and 'speaking' in a quite unusual and unmistakable voice.

When the day came for the bandage to be removed we had quite a shock: her foot came off in my hand. The Old Grey Hen however seemed greatly relieved. The sterile environment inside the bandage had allowed her stump to heal perfectly and as soon as she was replaced in her daybed she promptly walked off. I exaggerate here; she limped off, but so happy to have lost the dead weight on the end of her leg. She used her wings for balance and moved around at will, though still asking to be carried up steps and, to begin with, across the roadway to bed.

After a few weeks the end of her stump became sufficiently hardened to make her confident of crossing the concrete roadway herself. Sometimes she would fairly dash across before we could dream of intervening and sometimes she would stay on the soft lawn and require one of us to carry her. She knew whom she could trust.

After 48 years of keeping hens we finally had occasion to get involved in their everyday lives. Of all farm animals, hens are usually, if given freedom and access to a wide variety of food and lots of pure water, the most independent creatures and happy to be so. However these three learnt how to use us, to our delight and their benefit. The accident had happened in March but now that the hen was mobile she had the summer to look forward to. She hated to miss out on anything but whenever it rained she hid under the garden hammock and if the rain was heavy we brought her into the house. Her friends knew where she was and carried on as usual but when bedtime approached they simply would not go across the roadway to bed without her.

The Old Grey Hen soon accepted the situation; rain equals incarceration. I think she actually enjoyed the comfort. By now she was eating and drinking like a horse and apart from the noisy activity of pecking wheat from a container she was always silent until she decided it was time to go home. If one of us was close at hand she would only need to start manoeuvring towards the door to make her wishes clear. If, however, we were not handy she would resort to whatever tactics she thought necessary to attract our attention.

She would try her special speaking voice first: she had given up singing. Once, when that failed, she sidled over to the metal saucepan drawer under the cooker and banged louder and louder with her beak until we heard. We never kept her waiting again.

The Old Grey Hen enjoyed everything. She grazed the grass on the lawn voraciously; she investigated or dozed or weeded the rose bed; her friends scratched the earth with their feet and she ate whatever they turned up. Even when they had forgotten to be so polite about food allocation she could always beat them for speed with eye and beak, even if they could still run.

For 20 months The Old Grey Hen thrived but then came the day we had all been waiting for. She ate a modest breakfast but showed no interest in food at lunchtime. She seemed off-balance and hung her head. She died with her two close friends and two newer friends, whom we had bought a few months after her injury, by her side. The question of whether a hen can grieve had never previously occurred to us. The answer is 'yes'. We wondered whether the two bodyguards would miss their old friend but as we were to see during the succeeding days and weeks, all four were affected.

All the hens had appeared to be happy during the summer but we now know that they had restricted their activities to suit the Old Grey Hen's capabilities. They had turned into couch potatoes.

For the first few days after her death the four hens deliberately congregated in her erstwhile corner of the pen every night. After about a week they did some spring cleaning and we found to our surprise that the nest and the sack under it had been cleared away and the whole corner turned over and tidied. They were all subdued and shied away from human contact for some time. They also ate a great deal less.

Very gradually they began to resume active life and became more adventurous by the day. We would spot them in unaccustomed locations: down by the pond, in the yard with the cows, down behind the pig pens. Each day they roamed further afield, although we had felt certain that they had been happily suited to the confines of the garden. After three weeks they started laying eggs, resumed their friendly-to-human dispositions and insisted on staying up very late, talking and eating and playing in their pen for at least four hours longer than when the old girl had been one of their number."

# THE FOX AND SOME
# DISTURBING TALES

*Lynne Spencer from Beeston, Nottinghamshire writes:*

"Urban foxes can be a real problem to the hen keeper particularly when your neighbours buy frozen chickens to feed to the local fox population! We used to have a nightly visit from the local dog fox and indeed often a mid-morning and early evening visit too. On one occasion I looked out after dark to see the fox straddled across the apex of the hen house and I'm sure he was scratching his head wondering how on earth he could tempt them out for supper.

We always locked them up at night but he still made his visit on the off chance that we might have forgotten.

One hot summer evening I woke up to the sound of his barking and looked out of the bedroom window to see him sitting squarely at the side of the run. I banged on the window but to no avail; he merely acknowledged my presence by looking in my direction and then carried on with his vigil. I nudged my husband and suggested he got up and chased it off - but no! The chickens in the middle of the night were my responsibility (the same as the children had been funnily enough). Fox hunting wasn't his style!

Something had to be done. I didn't want my chickens terrorised so I decided to go down and confront the beast myself. I noisily opened the back door thinking that would send him on his way, but no he still sat there. There was nothing else for it. I was going to have to chase him off. I clapped my hands and walked gingerly towards him; after all I was bigger than him. He stood up stretched his legs glanced in my direction and settled down again. At this point I broke into a gallop and ran towards him only to be stopped dead in my tracks as I realised I had triggered the security light and I was stark naked and chasing a fox. At this point he ran off and I did a quick double take around the neighbours' windows to make sure I hadn't made a total exhibition of myself and confirmed what they already thought - that I was mad, and hiding my modesty with my hands as best I could I retreated back to the house.

I went back upstairs and told my husband what had happened and his response was classic. 'Well,' he said 'I'm not surprised he ran off - the sight of all that meat (referring to my ample frame) probably sent him off looking for reinforcements to help him tackle it.' With that he turned over and went back to sleep. So much for fox hunting! The fox continued to make nightly visits but I always made sure that on future forays I had a dressing gown handy if I was going out hunting - Hunting pink of course!"

*Ann Lloyd from Manchester writes:*

"I remember the fox once got in at night and ripped one of my girls' chests open, right down to the bone, trying to get her out of the ark. The vet said the shock would most likely kill her, she had antibiotics and lots of TLC and made a full recovery and lived another four years."

*Sarah White from Surrey writes:*

"I was woken yesterday morning about 6.30 by bird noises and looked out of the window to see my little grey bantam legging it down the garden. I rushed outside to where I have four very small bantams in a run. A fox had obviously forced the securing bar across the doors to get at the birds.

I then ran out to the road to check the fleeing bantam hadn't flown out of the garden, to see a fox with a bird in its mouth. I then searched a hedge and shrubbery for the little grey bantam but found nothing.

Returning to the run at the other end of the garden I found a dead Pekin and nearby a pile of black and white Sebright feathers.

Having broken the news to my son, we got on with breakfast and getting ready for a trip to London. We were both outside throwing balls for our dog about 8.30 when I went to check on water for the other hens and found the little grey bantam outside the run! I managed to corner her and return her to the run and went off to the garage to replenish her food. As I was opening the door, I suddenly saw the little Sebright at my feet!!! She had lost some breast feathers and had a small scratch but was otherwise OK.

The lessons I've learnt from this are:

Don't rely on swing closures for doors (a lot of hutches and arks have these); put on a bolt as well.
If you don't have a body, try and be about for a few hours in case any survivors emerge from hiding.
Heavily feathered birds are easy for the fox, it was my clean legged, nimble birds who escaped."

**Sally Hemming from Hampshire writes about losing some of her hybrids:**

"Two of our girls were killed during the afternoon about six weeks ago and since then the others are allowed into our two acre garden only with supervision, although I was around in and out of the garden on the day of the killing. Since then several times we had seen cubs literally playing in our garden during the day, so we asked a local gamekeeper to come round on Saturday and within 10 minutes he had shot one of the cubs. This was at about 7pm so it wasn't even dark. He said the others won't be back for a while but he'll come and do the business again should we have more sightings. I find it quite hard since I find it difficult to kill anything, but it has to be done to protect our girls. We must be a release site for urban foxes because one of the foxes shot last year had a long incision and stitch marks all the way up its leg and shoulder where it had obviously been "rescued" and released back into the wild!"

***Amy Dyson from Surrey writes:***

"Fox favourite seems to be duck first (as in duck - not interested in the drakes for some reason!) followed by hen (not cockerel - they definitely can tell the difference). I've only ever had one goose taken (again female, not male) and that was when the fox could creep up through the hay field.

Geese definitely will NOT protect other poultry - their reputation is much exaggerated. They are actually quite timid - although as with all things there will be the odd aggressive bird, especially in breeding season.

Our local gamekeeper has a saying - 'kill one fox and five come to the funeral'. Even if you get one fox there will be other rural foxes around which may be the cubs or the partner of the one you killed.

The other problem now which is making foxes unbearable is the 'rehoming' by townie idiots of urban foxes to the countryside for a 'nice new life' - yeah - until we can shoot or snare them - they are even worse than the rural foxes. Most rural foxes will still hunt more outside normal daylight hours - but the urban foxes are 24 x 7 killers.

You will never now be rid of foxes - all you can do is keep the population down to a level that ensures a balanced ecology by shooting/snaring/trapping/legal hunting. Current fox population is now reaching plague proportions, along with rats. Badgers in some areas are the same now that they are so protected.

I free range my birds and expect to perhaps lose one or two a year - which is the statistics for the last 10 years - but this year I have lost 10 due to released urban foxes and a local 'Wildlife Rescue' bunch who have been taking in fox cubs and releasing them near me. They even 'teach' the fox cubs to expect food at 3pm in the afternoon - the time they feed them - idiots - they don't give poultry keepers a chance.

At least if they wanted to rescue the damn things they could have the decency to feed them when it is dark so they learn to look for food at night.

At least the rescue centre has stopped releasing near me - found it a bit upsetting to think their nice little foxy rescue furry things ended up dead as quickly as I could shoot, snare or trap them.

Dogs are great as a protection and for the weeing - I refer to mine as being on 'chicken patrol' .

This year with the town foxes released, we've snared/trapped 15 so far and another was caught by the mower when the hay was cut. There have been literally dozens got by the gamekeeper as well - we're in a prime 'release' area for foxes trapped in London - most aggravating.

As with the explosion of the rat population in our cities, the potential for disease from all these urban foxes is a frightening thought."

***Vicky from Berkshire writes:***

"If you want the ultimate peace of mind then you have to protect your birds in a fox proof run or fencing. We have used poultry netting for six years and have had no foxes. It is excellent and is low maintenance. I have heard good things from others about this, too. Its initial set up is a little expensive but no more so that the heartbreak and price of replacement birds. Ours is mains powered but there are battery powered energisers, too."

*Finally, to end this book, here is an extract from a short story by Saki called THE SQUARE EGG which you may find amusing. Saki was the pseudonym for Hector Hugo Munro who was born in 1870 and died in 1916, shot by a sniper while serving as a Lance-Sergeant in the 22nd Royal Fusiliers.*

In the estaminet of the Fortunate Rabbit I found myself sitting next to an individual of indefinite age and nondescript uniform, who was obviously determined to make the borrowing of a match serve as a formal introduction and a banker's reference. He had the air of jaded jauntiness, the equipment of temporary amiability, the aspect of a foraging crow taught by experience to be wary and prompted by necessity to be bold; he had the contemplative downward droop of nose and moustache and the furtive sidelong range of eye – he had all those things that are the ordinary outfit of the purse-sapper the world over.

"I am a victim of the war," he exclaimed after a little preliminary conversation.

"One cannot make an omelette without breaking eggs," I answered, with the appropriate callousness of a man who had seen some dozens of square miles of devastated countryside and roofless homes.

"Eggs," he vociferated, "but it is precisely of eggs that I am about to speak. Have you ever considered what is the great drawback in the excellent and most useful egg – the ordinary, every day egg of commerce and cookery?"

"Its tendency to age rapidly is sometimes against it," I hazarded; "Unlike the United States of North America which grow more respectable and self-respecting the longer they last, an egg gains nothing by persistence; it resembles your Louis the Fifteenth, who declined in popular favour with every year he lived – unless the historians have entirely misrepresented his record."

"No," replied the Tavern Acquaintance seriously, "It is not a question of age. It is the shape, the roundness. Consider how easily it rolls. On a table, a shelf, a shop counter, perhaps, one little push, and it may roll to the floor and be destroyed. What catastrophe for the poor, the frugal!"

I gave a sympathetic shudder at the idea; eggs here cost 6 sous apiece.

"Monsieur," he continued, "It is a subject I had often pondered and turned over in my mind, this economical malformation of the household egg. In our little village of Verchey-les-Torteaux, in the Department of the Tarn, my aunt has a small dairy and poultry farm, from which we drew a modest income. We were not poor, but there was always the necessity to labour, to contrive, to be sparing. One day I chanced to notice that one of my aunt's hens, a hen of the mop-headed Houdan breed, had laid an egg that was not altogether so round-shaped as the eggs of other hens; it could not be called square, but it had well-defined angles. I found out that this particular bird always laid eggs of this particular shape. The discovery gave a new stimulus to my ideas. If one collected all the hens that one could find with a tendency to lay a slightly angular egg and bred chickens only from those hens, and went on selecting and selecting, always choosing those that laid the squarest egg, at last, with patience and enterprise, one would produce a breed of fowls that laid only square eggs."

"In the course of several hundred years one might arrive at such a result," I said; "it would more probably take several thousands."

"With your cold Northern conservative slow-moving hens that might be the case," said the Acquaintance impatiently and rather angrily; "with our vivacious Southern poultry it is different. Listen. I searched, I experimented, I explored the poultry yards of our neighbours, I ransacked the markets of the surrounding towns, wherever I found a hen laying an angular egg I bought her; I collected in time a vast concourse of fowls all sharing the same tendency; from their progeny I selected only those pullets whose eggs showed the most marked deviation from the normal roundness. I continued, I persevered. Monsieur, I produced a breed of hens that laid an egg which could not roll, however much you might push or jostle it. My experiment was more than a success; it was one of the romances of modern industry."

Of that I had not the least doubt, but I did not say so.

"My eggs became known," continued the soi-distant poultry farmer; "at first they were sought after as a novelty, something curious, bizarre. Then merchants and housewives began to see that they were a utility, an improvement, an advantage over the ordinary kind. I was able to command a sale for my wares at a price considerably above market rates. I began to make money. I had a monopoly. I refused to sell any of my "square-layers" and the eggs that went to market were carefully sterilised, so that no chickens should be hatched from them. I was on the way to becoming rich, comfortably rich. Then this war broke out, which has brought misery to so many. I was obliged to leave my hens and my customers and go to the Front. My aunt carried on the business as usual, sold the square eggs, the eggs that I had devised and created and perfected and received the profits; can you imagine it, she refused to send me one centime of the takings! She says that she looks after the hens, and pays for their corn and sends the eggs to market and that the money is hers. Legally, of course, it is mine; if I could afford to bring a process in the courts I could recover all the money that the eggs have brought in since the war commenced, many thousands of francs. To bring a process would only need a small sum; I have a lawyer friend who would arrange matters cheaply for me. Unfortunately I have not sufficient  funds in hand; I need still about 80 francs. In wartime alas, it is difficult to borrow."

I had always imagined that it was a habit that was especially indulged in during wartime and said so.

"On a big scale, yes but I am talking of a very small matter. It is easier to arrange a loan of millions than of a trifle of 80 or 90 francs."

The would-be financier paused for a few tense moments. Then he recommenced in a more confident strain. "Some of you English soldiers, I have heard, are men with private means: is it not so? It is perhaps possible that among your comrades there might be someone willing to advance a small sum – you yourself, perhaps – it would be a secure and profitable investment, quickly repaid."

"If I get a few days' leave I will go down to Verchey-les-Torteaux and inspect the square-egg-hen-farm," I said gravely, "And question the local egg-merchants as to the position and prospects of the business."

The Tavern Acquaintance gave an almost imperceptible shrug to his shoulders, shifted in his seat and began moodily to roll a cigarette. His interest in me had suddenly died out, but for the sake of appearances he was bound to make a perfunctory show of winding up the conversation he had so laboriously started.

"Ah, you will go the Verchy-les-Torteaux and make enquiries about our farm. And if you find that what I have told you about the square eggs is true, Monsieur, what then?"

"I shall marry your aunt."